# A Narrative of
# the Military Actions of
# Colonel Marinus Willett
# William W. Willett

The New York Times & Arno Press

# A

# NARRATIVE

OF

# THE MILITARY ACTIONS

OF

## COLONEL MARINUS WILLETT,

TAKEN CHIEFLY FROM HIS OWN MANUSCRIPT.

---

PREPARED BY HIS SON, WILLIAM M. WILLETT.

New-York:

PUBLISHED BY G. & C. & H. CARVILL.

1831.

---

LUDWIG & TOLEFREE, PRINTERS.

# DEDICATION.

———»+●◉●+«———

TO GENERAL LA FAYETTE,

SIR,

The following pages contain a plain and un-
adorned narrative of the principal military actions in
which Col. Willett was engaged during the French
and Revolutionary wars : together with an account
of his Mission to the Creek Indians. The whole
narrative is little more than a transcript of what he
himself wrote, after he had attained his seventieth
year. In it, will be found a few incidents of an interesting nature, connected with our Revolutionary
war, which heretofore have been but slightly, if at
all, touched by the pen of the traveller or the histo-
rian : while the circumstances that these pages contain the otherwise perishing memorials of one of our
oldest Revolutionary Soldiers, will, it is hoped, impart to them a peculiar interest.

## DEDICATION.

Allow me, Sir, in giving this narrative to the public, to dedicate it to you, as one of those few surviving patriots who connect past struggles with present triumph and prosperity : and one, for whom Colonel Willett entertained the highest esteem, and the warmest sentiments of friendship.

I remain,

Sir,

with sentiments of great respect,

**WILLIAM M. WILLETT.**

*New-York, August 15th,* 1831.

# TABLE OF CONTENTS.

—◦◦●◎●◦◦—

## CHAPTER I.

# CONTENTS.

## CHAPTER VII.

# CHAPTER I.

—••+⊕⊕⊕+••—

## INTRODUCTORY REMARKS.

THE Revolutionary War, though an event not sufficiently remote to produce that mingled feeling of awe and veneration with which we regard great occurrences that have long since transpired, is still of not so recent date, but that time already begins to throw a deeper shade of interest over the numerous and remarkable transactions which distinguish that eventful period. The banks of the Delaware : the plains of Saratoga and of Monmouth : the environs of York-town ; grow dearer to us with the lapse of years ; and as the course of time renders the actions which were performed on these memorable spots still more and more remote, our admiration will continue to increase : until, like the plains of Marathon, and the straits of Thermopylæ, they will be viewed as classic ground by every lover of civil freedom. They will be spoken of with veneration : they will be approached with the deepest interest : while the recollections of former achievements, consecrating these hallowed scenes, will awaken within the bosom the liveliest feelings of emulation and patriotism.

This war, of so much importance to the future welfare of our country, was peculiarly distinguished for the patriotism which was displayed throughout every stage of the protracted and arduous struggle. Acting from an enlightened

conviction of their just rights : suppressing rather than giving way to the full burst of indignation which would natu-
rally arise in generous minds from unmerited oppression,—
the patriots of the Revolution proceeded to take their pre-
liminary measures with the utmost coolness, deliberation,
and firmness : and when they discovered that it was utterly
impossible to adjust existing differences without relinquish-
ing rights which were esteemed essential to the enjoyment
of liberty, they then pledged themselves not to abandon a
cause with which they conceived their own honour and
happiness, and that of their posterity, to be forever after
inseparably connected. Engaging thus in so important a
cause, from a clear conviction of its justice, and not merely
from a sense of oppression, they displayed a spirit of steady
resistance to the most vigorous efforts of their powerful and
inveterate adversary. They were undismayed by misfortune ; undaunted by numbers. They rose with every re-
verse of fortune ; and plucked the laurels of victory almost
in the very moment of defeat. Unsubdued by every variety
of suffering, they would have preferred retiring beyond the
Alleghany, rather than to have submitted to the government
of their oppressors. In the midst of portending ruin, their
valour and patriotism, confined to neither rank nor place,
opened a way for their deliverance, and ultimately crowned
their efforts with complete success.

Among the number of those brave patriots, who espoused
the cause of freedom, fought in her ranks, and were ready
to lay down their lives in defence of her violated rights,
Colonel Willett was not the least zealous. It is true he
was engaged in but few of the principal actions throughout
the war. The battle of Monmouth was the only general
action in which he took a part, and in this he served as a
volunteer. It was his fortune to be stationed chiefly on the

frontiers; but perhaps this very circumstance may heighten the interest of his services. To the more prominent events of the Revolution, little or nothing remains to be added; but as its leading outlines are filled up and crowded with facts, many a feat of gallantry may still be gleaned from this rich field of adventure, heretofore in part or wholly hidden, on account, perhaps, of their remoteness from the principal scene of action. Indeed, it is the enterprising and intrepid valour which Colonel Willett displayed, in rude and wild scenes of warfare, which has encircled his name, in the annals of his country, with an imperishable wreath of glory. His sortie from Fort Stanwix; his passing afterwards, through the enemy's camp, in company with Major Stockwell, and traversing the wilderness for fifty miles, exposed every instant to a cruel and enraged foe, have been the theme of high encomium even by British historians. His services along the Mohawk river, the entire security which he afforded to that rich frontier settlement, were considered of great utility and importance by General Washington and Governor Clinton, and are perhaps remembered to this day by a few of the old inhabitants.

As a patriot, I do not think my filial love and veneration will incur censure, for having led me into extravagant praise, when I say that no man could love his country with more intense affection. Enlisting in her service early on the morning of that day, so lowering and overcast with clouds, it was plain that the risk he ran, in common with others, was forgotten in the love he entertained for his country, and in a feeling of indignation against those who would have oppressed her, and robbed her of her rights. In the very commencement of the contest he was anxious to take a part so bold and decided, that all hope of compromise, so far as he was personally concerned, should be cut off.

Throughout every stage of the arduous struggle, his heart remained true to the cause of freedom, and it was not until peace was proclaimed that he laid down his arms.

At the close of the war, Colonel Willett returned to civil pursuits. Under the administration of General Washington, he negotiated terms of peace between the Creek nation and the United States ; an event in which General Washington was deeply interested.

In addition to negotiating this treaty, Colonel Willett filled several other civil offices; and after his retirement from public life, he frequently appeared among his fellow-citizens, on interesting occasions, always manifesting a lively interest in the honour and prosperity of his country.

Thus he lived, growing old amidst the esteem and affections of his fellow-citizens ; and as time continually diminished the number of his old associates in arms, becoming like one of a few noble trees of a once large and flourishing forest, more and more an object of respect and veneration.

At length Colonel Willett sunk under the weight of years. The numerous public testimonials to his character, and the tribute of respect paid to his remains, by an immense concourse of his fellow-citizens, showed the degree of honour in which in his old age, and in the retirement of private life, he was still held.

> "So sleep the brave, who sink to rest
> By all their country's honours blest."

All that now remains to his country, is the recollection of his services in her cause ; his ardent attachment to her welfare. And having devoted the fulness and strength of his days, to promote the glory and prosperity of his country, his name perhaps will not soon be forgotten, but in a later period still of her history, be found adorning some page in the annals of that eventful period in which he lived.

# CHAPTER II.

—⁕⊛⊛⊛⁕—

COLONEL Marinus Willett was born on the 31st of July,
(old style) 1740, in Jamaica, Long Island, in the State of
New York. He was of a respectable family: his grand-
father Samuel Willett, held the office of Sheriff of Queen's
county, Long Island: his father, Edward Willett, born in
the year 1701, lived on a farm on the island a number of
years, though he afterwards removed to New York, where
he continued to reside until his death. He died in his son's
house at the advanced age of 93.

Colonel Willett was one of thirteen children: he survived
them all. Elbert Willett, who died at his residence in Albany a few years since, at the age of 90, was, with the exception of Colonel Willett, the sole surviving member of the
family. Of six brothers, of whom Colonel Willett was the
youngest, but one besides himself engaged in either the
colonial or revolutionary war: this was Isaac, the fourth
brother, who went as a lieutenant in a privateer in the French
war, in the year '58, was cast away in a hurricane, and,
with all on board, perished.

Colonel Willett was between fifteen and sixteen years of
age, when an impressment took place in the city of New
York, which was the first circumstance of a public nature
that left a serious impression on his mind. The follow-

2

ing is his own account of the transaction. "A number of marines belonging to the English men-of-war, then lying in the harbour, were employed in impressing men for those ships. They commenced their business very early in the morning; and though it was afterwards said that their orders were to impress only such as had the appearance of sea-faring or labouring men, yet several respectable citizens were seized by those press-gangs, who scrupled not to enter into whatsoever house they pleased, without regarding the ter-ror or protestations of the occupants. Such was the conduct of the British government in this City, at a time when the least disloyalty would have been deemed an unpardonable offence : strange as it may appear, these outrages upon the inhabitants were perpetrated without the shadow of oppo-sition."

In the year '58, a great degree of military excitement per-vaded the colonies, in consequence of the vigorous efforts of Mr. Pitt, to retrieve the losses and disgrace which had attended the British arms for several preceding campaigns in the war, which at that period raged with great violence, be-tween France and Great Britain. Colonel Willett, prompted by the ardour of youth, and fired by a natural enthusiasm, caught the general flame ; and a relation of the family who was in the public service, offering his assistance to procure him a commission in the army, he eagerly embraced the offer : shortly after, he received a second lieutenant's com-mission in a colonial regiment.

The regiment with which Colonel Willett was con-nected had been raised in the colony of New-York. It consisted of three battalions of nine hundred men each ; and was commanded by Oliver Delancy, brother to James Delancy, at that time Lieutenant Governor of the colony of New-York. The company to which Colonel Willett was attached, was composed of men raised on Long Island, and was placed under the command of Thomas Williams, a man of activity and courage.

Colonel Willett has left the following description of the dress which, as a lieutenant, he wore upon this his youthful campaign. It may be gratifying to those who are fond of the most common reliques of past times, to preserve it in this place. It consisted of a green coat, trimmed with silver twist, white under clothes and black gaiters; also a cocked hat, with a large black cockade of silk ribbon, together with a silver button and loop.

Thus equipped, between the age of seventeen and eighteen, on the seventh of May, Lieutenant Willett left New-York with his regiment. Upon the arrival of the regiment at Albany, orders were received to march up the Mohawk river, in order to guard the settlements which had already been formed along that rich tract of country, against the incursions of the French and Indians. The march from Albany to Schenectady was the first he ever made; and as the day was warm, and the road sandy, he was excessively fatigued; more so, he says, than upon any other march, though he afterwards made many a heavy and fatiguing one.

After remaining for the space of two weeks as a guard to the inhabitants along the river, the regiment was ordered to join the main army, under General Abercrombie, commander-in-chief, which was assembling at the south end of Lake George. Arriving at the general place of rendezvous, the utmost activity was found to prevail throughout every department of the army, owing chiefly to the spirited exertions of the gallant and amiable Howe. This most promising and heroic English nobleman, appears to have quickly gained the universal esteem and affection of the army. His manners were easy; his carriage unassuming; his dress very plain. In the midst of the most unceasing activity in receiving and inspecting the troops, disciplining them, introducing a reform in their dress, and looking into the minutiæ of every department of the army, his deportment was uniformly gentle and modest. In fine, the ability and industry which he displayed, marked him out, to use Colonel Willett's expression, as the life and soul of the army—as the individual upon whose exertions the success of the campaign mainly depended.

The diligence and activity with which the necessary preparations were made, enabled the commander-in-chief to open the campaign at an early period in the season: a circumstance of the utmost importance, as perhaps to this cause was owing the utter failure of several preceding campaigns. Accordingly, on the fifth day of June, soon after day-break, the army, consisting of sixteen thousand troops, embarked in batteaux, whale-boats, and flats, and proceeded with much beauty and regularity along the Lake.*

At sunset the troops reached a place called Sabaday's Point, where they landed. Fires were lighted along the shore, as far as the troops extended. Here the army remained until midnight; when, re-embarking and pursuing their course, they arrived at the north end of the Lake, at the dawn of day. At this spot the enemy had a post : the landing of the army was however effected with but a slight opposition ; and the troops formed along the

---

* This passage across Lake George is thus described in Dr. Dwight's Travels : " On the fifth the whole army, except a reserve, left for the protection of this spot, embarked in a thousand and thirty-five boats, with all the splendour of military parade. The morning was remarkably bright and beautiful; and the fleet moved with exact regularity to the sound of fine martial music : the ensigns waved and glittered in the sunbeams ; and the anticipation of future triumph shone in every eye ; above, beneath, around, the scenery was that of enchantment ; and rarely has the sun, since that luminary was first lighted up in the heavens, dawned on such a complication of beauty and magnificence."

margin of the shore in good order, and with expedition. Two French regular soldiers who happened to lie near where Lieutenant Willett landed, were the first persons he ever saw scalped. They were killed in the slight rencontre that ensued at the disembarkation of the troops ; and their scalps were taken off by some Indians of the Stockbridge tribe, who crossed the Lake with the army.

After a short halt, the troops began to move towards Ticonderoga through woods in columns by regiments. Good order prevailed throughout the army ; and the prospect of success was flattering.

The eve of battle is a moment of breathless anxiety ; not perhaps always unmixed with fear. Colonel Willett preserved a distinct recollection of his feelings when about to engage for the first time in battle. He says, that neither at this time, nor upon any subsequent occasion, did he experience the least degree of fear. On the contrary, he uniformly found his spirits elated, as the crisis approached. And that now, when expecting every instant to come in contact with the enemy, though young and unacquainted with danger, his spirits were highly exhilarated.

The army had not proceeded above two miles on their march, when an ambush of the enemy was discovered, not far from the column in which Lieutenant Willett marched. Lord Howe was soon in front of the column. But at the very moment when this gallant officer had placed himself in a most conspicuous situation, and was employed in animating the troops, he received a shot which put an instant period to his life. Thus fell this interesting nobleman. The ambuscade was formed principally of French regular troops, said to be under one thousand, who were soon dispersed, killed or made prisoners. But the confusion which followed this unexpected attack was extremely great : indeed after the death of Lord Howe the troops in general seemed to be destitute of command. Wandering parties from different quarters were firing on each other when there was not an enemy to be found. The shaking of a leaf would set a whole line of troops firing, and frequently running. In one instance, through a false alarm, upwards of a thousand men, including officers, ran into the river, where they were in danger of drowning.

This disorder continued throughout the remainder of the day. The different corps intermixed with each other; and the whole army was little better than a wandering rabble, moving from place to place, without appearing to have any definite object in view. Not an officer of distinction appeared to direct their movements.

During this state of disorder, Lieutenant Willett connected himself with one Muncey, an Irishman by birth, an adjutant in his regiment, and who had seen regular service. The exertions of this officer, together with his commanding appearance, enabled him to collect several hundred men in a body, of whom he assumed the command. With the utmost difficulty these men were made to move in tolerable order. While this party were pursuing their devious course through the woods, they accidentally fell in with the commander-in-chief. The poor old gentleman was standing under a huge tree, wrapped in a large cloak, with two regular regiments drawn up around him to defend his person. This was the only instance in which Lieutenant Willett saw troops under regular command, after the disorder occasioned by the first attack. One would be ready to suppose that the body of troops with which Lieutenant Willett was connected, having fallen in with the commander-in-chief, would have received directions for their movements; but no orders were given, and they continued to wander about among the woods, under the idea of clearing them of the enemy, until night overtook them. They halted when they could no longer see ; then wrapping themselves up in the best manner they were able, they lay down close together in order to keep each other warm. The fatigue and weariness of the day, and having had no sleep the preceding night, soon threw Lieut. Willett into a deep sleep ; so that he passed the night with some degree of comfort. On rising in the morning, he perceived that his party had passed the night near the spot where the action commenced, as a number of naked corpses were lying around them.

It was ten o'clock in the morning before Muncey with his party reached the place. of their former landing. The greater part of the troops had arrived at this place before them. It was past noon before the army recommenced their march towards Ticonderoga. When within three miles of the Fort, they halted, and encamped for the night in the woods, without tents.

Early the following morning, the army was increased by the arrival of about six hundred Indians, under the command of Sir William Johnson. These Indians crossed the river, and went on the hill opposite the Fort, where they made a great yelling and firing, which appears to have been a needless manœuvre, for they could hardly hope by this course to intimidate the enemy, as they were perfectly familiar with the Indian yell and war-whoop.

By nine o'clock in the morning, every part of this large and well-furnished army was in motion. The regiment with which Lieutenant Willett was connected, moved in files towards Lake Champlain, intending to strike the lake between the Fort and Crown Point, at a distance of two miles from the Fort. On their march, they fell in with other bodies of troops, who appeared to be at a loss respecting the

ground they were ordered to occupy, for the want of expé-
rienced guides. It was just noon, when the guide who had
undertaken to direct the regiment to which Lieut. Willett belonged, conceiving that he was too far to the left,
inclined suddenly to the right. Lieut. Willett was with the
advanced guard of his regiment, when some French regulars
were discovered in a thicket, who, on being challenged, began
to run, when they were fired at and pursued. In the eagerness of pursuit the regiment became entangled among fallen
trees; and at that moment, a cleared field opening to their
view, they saw the enemy striking their tents. Endeavouring still to advance, with all possible expedition, they were
suddenly checked by a very heavy fire of musketry and
grape-shot. It was then for the first time discovered, that
they were directly under the enemy's breast-work; and that
the fallen trees were intended as abbatis. Though taken by
surprise, the regiment supported their ground, by returning
as effective a fire as was in their power. In a short time
several regiments were seen moving towards the enemy's
works on their right. The regiments which Lieut. Willett
noticed particularly, were the 55th, Gage's light infantry,
and the Highland Watch. These troops moved on very
rapidly, until they became entangled among the fallen trees;
when they made sudden halts, and commenced an ineffectual firing.

The greater part of the army appeared now to be engaged
in endeavouring to force the enemy's works. In the meanwhile the enemy's fire was doing immense execution. The
English and Colonial troops fell in every direction, while,
to add to their mortification, it was impossible for them,
under their present mode of attack, without artillery, to
make the least impression upon the enemy. The troops
laboured also under another difficulty in consequence of

the order in which they marched. In the exercise then in use, a file consisted of three men : one filing to what was termed the front, one the centre, and one the rear rank. In such files, the troops marched to the attack. They were, therefore, not in a condition to support each other, neither were they able to force the enemy's works. Some of the troops, where the abbatis were not so thick, advanced close to the enemy's breast work ; and a few individuals, with the utmost gallantry, mounted them : but not being sufficiently supported, they were instantly cut down, or made prisoners. This was the case with the sergeant major of Lieut. Willett's regiment, who was taken prisoner, and carried to Canada ; and with whom Lieut. Willett conversed after his release.

In the mean while, the ranks of the British and the colonists continued to lessen very fast. The wounded were every moment carried off : the dead strewed the ground. A severe firing was kept up upwards of five hours ; and it was near sun-set before it entirely ceased. The troops withdrew without order, and night overtook them before they were able to carry off all their wounded.

Lieutenant Willett's inexperience rendered him entirely ignorant of what was next to be done. Under the impression that the Fort was to be taken at all hazards ; and having that morning seen some heavy artillery moving in flats, along the shore, he drew the conclusion, that another attack was to be made the next day, aided by heavy artillery. With this expectation, and being very much fatigued, he retired with about thirty men of his regiment to a hill, not above a mile distant from the ground where the attack was first made. Here they kindled a fire, and having collected some canteens of water and a few biscuits, they refreshed themselves and lay down to rest. A number of fires, lighted in various directions around them, showed that

3

others were following their example, and, after the fatigues
and perils of the day, were retiring for repose.

In a few minutes Lieut. Willett was fast asleep. He was
awakened before morning by some one pulling him violently,
and informing him, that the troops were already on their
march back to the place of landing. He, of course, with
the rest of his company, set out for the old spot, by making
towards the river, and then keeping near its shore. They
reached the landing about eight o'clock in the morning, and
found the troops embarking in a very confused manner. As
there was no enemy to interrupt them, all the troops who
arrived, were placed in safety on board the boats. But as to
the wounded, some were left in the woods, and no inconsiderable number in the field where the action occurred, not
far from the enemy's works.

This last fact was fully proved by subsequent accounts.
Among others, a very tragical one respecting Colonel Beaver,
who was a lieutenant colonel in a regular British regiment.
He was a young gentleman of a distinguished family in
England : much respected and beloved. His loss was
greatly lamented ; and he was supposed to have been killed
in the action. But it afterwards appeared, that he remained
on the field badly wounded ; and was discovered the morning after the action, by a French officer, who was sent out
with a small detachment to reconnoitre. Colonel Beaver
was sitting on the stump of a tree when the party came
along ; and having made himself known to the French
officer, requested to be taken under his protection. The
officer informed him that this was not in his power, until he
had gone to the top of a hill, not more than a hundred yards
distant : he assured him, however, that upon his return,
which would be in a very short time, he might depend upon his protection, and upon a safe conveyance to the Fort.

The officer, however, had proceeded but a short distance, when, hearing a cry, he turned around and saw an Indian scalping the unfortunate colonel. It was said that the officer, upon his return, informed the French commandant, General Montcalm, of this distressing case; and endeavoured to have the Indian, who perpetrated the deed, punished, on the ground that the Indian was present, and witnessed the surrender of Colonel Beaver. But Montcalm replied, "that in their situation it would not do to offend the Indians."*

In such haste and confusion did the English army retreat, after the failure of the ill-concerted attack upon the Fort at Ticonderoga. This retreat was the more ignominious, for though General Abercrombie had sustained a loss of nearly two thousand men in killed and wounded, yet there still remained fourteen thousand effective troops: a force so much superior to that of the enemy that there was no reason

---

* A piece of poetry which appeared some time after this disaster in a British Magazine, and which was said to have been enclosed in a letter to the father of Col. Beaver, made such an impression on Col. Willett's mind as induced him to commit it to memory. The reader perhaps will be pleased to see it in this place.

"Tell me," says Cato, "where you found
  "My boy; and how he fell?
"In front;—and in his breast the wound.
  "I thank the gods,—'tis well.
"Thus the stern Stoic sooth'd his grief,
  "And check'd the rising moan,
"By making honour his relief,
  "And common good his own."

"May you on such reflections dwell,
  When you behold this urn;
And as he like a Roman fell,
  So like a Roman mourn.

"True he was young, and brave as young,
  And generous as brave;
Yet every virtue could not long
  Or him, or Marius save.

"Save not even Howe, in arms so great,
  By all admired, adored;
While nations trembled at the fate
  Depending on his sword."

to apprehend an attack from them, while the remaining force was sufficiently large to invest the Fort. Reinforcements too might undoubtedly have been obtained if necessary : so that a siege might with safety have been commenced, which, if conducted with any degree of vigour, would soon have compelled the garrison to surrender. But to abandon the project altogether, and to retreat in so precipitate and disorderly a manner, leaving a number of brave men wounded to be cruelly sacrificed, evinced such terror as must have destroyed for a time even the power of reflection.*

The army having safely re-crossed the Lake, landed at the south end of it, early in the evening, where they encamped on their former ground.

The day after the army had returned to their encampment, the regiment to which Lieut. Willett belonged, received orders to march up the Mohawk river ; and in about two weeks they arrived at the portage, between the waters of the Mohawk and Ontario, at the head of Wood Creek. At this place an army of about six thousand men was assembled, under the command of General Stanwix ; and a plan was laid out for a fort, which was afterwards erected, and called Fort Stanwix.

It was evident that preparations were making for a secret expedition. Parties were employed in erecting a dam at the head of Wood Creek ; conveying batteaux and provisions to the same place ; and removing various obstructions to the navigation of the stream. These measures were conducted with great despatch by Colonel Bradstreet, who in two weeks from the time of his arrival at the portage, commenced his march with about three thousand men. The

---

* See Appendix, No. 1.

whole of this force consisted of provincial troops, with the exception of one independent regular company, commanded by Captain Ogilvie; and a company of artillery, under the command of Captain Stevens. One thousand men were chosen from the regiment to which Lieut. Willett belonged, to be employed in this expedition. The captain of his company remaining behind, he was annexed with thirty men to another company, commanded by Captain Thomas Arrowsmith, an active, good officer.

Colonel Bradstreet, who commanded this expedition, was well qualified for the enterprise: the success of which depended very much upon the celerity of his movements. The troops passed down Wood Creek with all the expedition in their power, though they were greatly impeded by the lowness of the water, and obstructions occasioned by trees, which the year before had been felled across the Creek by order of General Webb, after the loss of Fort William Henry: a measure which savoured more of timidity than skill.

Although Colonel Bradstreet used the greatest exertion, yet six days elapsed before he reached Oswego. At this place he remained a few hours, inspecting the troops, their arms and ammunition, and repairing the injuries the boats had received in their portage at the falls, and passage down the rapids. It was near dusk when the troops embarked on board vessels, provided to transport them over Lake Ontario. Keeping near the shore of the Lake during the night, on account of the danger to which the boats would be exposed by crossing at a distance from the land, caused some delay, so that they did not arrive in sight of Fort Frontinac, the place of destination, until the evening of the third day, after leaving Oswego.

They landed in the night, within two miles of the Fort. The day following, the greater part of the men were em- ployeb in the woods, in making gabions and fascines. During this day, their ordnance, consisting of two small mortars, was also landed, and having been erected about three quarters of a mile from the Fort, shells were fired at intervals, the greater part of the day. The enemy also kept up a constant .fire from the Fort; but their fire as well as ours was without effect. Towards evening, the enemy had the misfortune to blow up one of their magazines, by which a breach was made in one of their bastions.

Shortly after it was dark, a detachment of nine hun- dred men marched towards the Fort. Every man had a bundle of fascines in his hand, or every two men carried between them a gabion on a pole. Advancing in this order, through a hollow way, they took possession of a small eminence, only a hundred and seventy-five yards from the Fort, where they commenced the erection of a breastwork, with two embrasures. Colonel Bradstreet was himself present when this work was laid out, and remained to inspect its progress, until it was in a state of considerable forwardness. Five hundred men of the regiment with which Lieut. Willett was connected, were chosen for this service, and placed under the command of Lieut. Colonel Curea. Lieut. Willett, whose fortune it was to be placed in exposed points during the various scenes of the campaign, was one of this detachment. The unavoidable noise, occa- sioned by the erection of these works, soon discovered to the enemy what was going on, who directed against them a cor- stant fire of grape-shot and musketry during the whole of the night. Such, however, was the diligence and celerity which had been used during the night, that by day-light, the breastwork was sufficiently high to cover the men, together with two brass twelve-pounders. As soon as the cannon were mounted, a fire was commenced against the Fort, and kept up as briskly as possible. A brig which lay under the Fort got under sail, but was soon made to run on shore by the fire of a few shot from the twelve-pounders. By nine o'clock the beating of the chamade by the enemy brought on a parley, which terminated in a surrender of the garrison with all its contents before twelve o'clock at noon. The enemy who were made prisoners of war, were suffered to go into Canada on the promise of the commandant to send an equal number in exchange.*

The afternoon of the day on which the Fort was taken, was spent in destroying the works, sending off the most valuable articles, setting fire to the buildings, blowing up the magazines, and burning all the vessels of the enemy, (of which they had nine) with the exception of two, in which had been deposited the most valuable articles taken from the Fort. The design of the expedition being thus accomplished, the detachment set out on its return, having lost but one man, and eleven wounded, but none of them dangerously. They proceeded to the island where they halted when they first came in view of the Fort. Early the next morning all the troops were on board the boats on their way back to Oswego. At Oswego the batteaux were loaded with the goods which had been placed in the enemy's vessels: after which the vessels themselves were set on fire. The troops then proceeded with as much expedition as possible to Oswego Falls.

At Oswego Falls they had a portage of a mile or more.

* Appendix, No. 2.

The excessive fatigue of getting the boats, stores, and goods across the carrying place, at this portage, added to the great exertions they had already undergone, and the short time allowed for cooking their provisions, consisting of pork and flour, had produced violent dysenteries. Unaccustomed to such fare, and without proper stores or attendance, the men began to die very fast. During the three days that the men were employed in dragging the boats up the rapids, and carrying them across the portage, there were near one hundred deaths. And by the time the troops arrived at Fort Bull, which was four miles from the place where they were building Fort Stanwix, at least one half of their number were unfit for duty. Removing the boats into the Mohawk river, and carrying the goods over the portage, was a work of four days.

Here ended with Lieut. Willett the active part of this campaign. On the night of his arrival at Fort Stanwix, in consequence of the incessant fatigue and exposure, which with the rest he had sustained on this last expedition, he was taken very ill; and confined to a tent in the camp until the begining of November. Having gained a little strength, he was put on board a batteau, and after a most painful journey of three days, arrived at Schenectady; from thence he was conveyed to Albany. Here he remained at the house of Mr. Sullivan, by whom he was most hospitably entertained, until the first of December. The weather having become more moderate, and the river which had been frozen over having broken up, he commenced his passage for New-York; where he arrived early on the morning of the seventh, having been just seven months from home.

In consequence however of the feeble state of Lieut. Willett's health, after his return home, together with the disinclination of his parents, he did not serve any more during the French war.   Indeed, the great success which followed the British arms in Europe as well as in North America the two ensuing years, brought about a speedy peace between France and England.   The campaign, however, was not wholly without its use to Lieut. Willett, as it gave him some insight into a mode of warfare, in which at a late period of his life he was peculiarly successful.

# CHAPTER III.

—————

In the regular British army, left in America, and quartered in the greater part of the large cities and towns, after the close of the French war, we see proofs of the design of the English ministry on the colonists. It appeared, that the army which had been sent over to the Colonies, to protect them from a foreign foe, and in conjunction with which force, the colonists themselves had very materially aided in obtaining important conquests for the British government, was now in its turn to be employed, in forcing the assent of the Colonies to unconstitutional taxation. The measures of the ministry soon discovered their hostile intentions, and excited the vigilance of the citizens. The memorable Stamp Act, which followed, met with the most determined opposition. In the city of New York, the inhabitants assembled in a very tumultuous manner. Several persons, who had been particularly instrumental in procuring the passage of that obnoxious measure, were hung in effigy, and then burnt. The citizens burnt also the governor's coach, and entering the dwelling of Colonel James, the officer who commanded the troops, at that time quartered in the city, and who, with the governor, had shut himself up in the Fort, they destroyed all the furniture found in his house. The person who had been employed to issue the stamped paper, was obliged to enter into the most solemn engagements not to act under the appointment. The tumult continued to rage for several days; nor did it subside, until the most satisfactory assurances were obtained, from all persons suspected of having any agency in supporting, or executing the act, that they would desist from the execution of it, and join in an application for a repeal of the law. In the mean time, all law proceedings were suspended, and a total stagnation of every kind of business ensued, which could not legally be pursued without the use of stamped paper.

Similar acts of opposition and violence breaking out, in every part of the Union, procured, as is well known, a sudden repeal of that obnoxious measure. A variety of methods were, however, afterwards devised, by the British parliament, to force a revenue from the Colonies, which finally resulted in the battle of Lexington.

The news of this memorable event was received at New York, the Sunday after it took place, and occasioned a general insurrection. The people assembled; and finding themselves unable to procure the key of an arsenal, where a number of arms belonging to the colonial government were deposited, they forced open the door, and took possession of these arms. By taking this course, they procured about six hundred muskets, with bayonets and cartridge-boxes to each, filled with ball-cartridges. These arms were distributed among the most active of the citizens, who formed themselves into a voluntary corps, and assumed the government of the city. They took possession of the keys of the custom-house, together with all the public stores. There was a general stagnation of business. The armed citizens were constantly parading about the city, without seeming to have any defi-

nite object in view. Part of the eighteenth British regiment, called the Royal Irish, garrisoned in the city, and
under the command of the major of the regiment, confined
themselves to their barracks.

The unsystematic manner, however, in which measures
were conducted, shewed the necessity of forming some regular plan of government. To accomplish this object, a meeting
of the citizens was called at the Merchants' Coffee House,
where it was unanimously agreed, that the government
should be placed in the hands of a committee. At the
same time, solemn resolutions were entered into, to support
the measures of the committee, until further provision
should be made by the continental congress. The sacred
honor of the citizens was also pledged to support the measures of congress.

This committee was limited to one hundred ; and being
instantly chosen, and entering upon the discharge of their
duties, restored as much order in the city, as, under circumstances so new and extraordinary, could reasonably be expected. As however in the city of New-York, at this time,
there was a very large portion of personal influence in favour
of the British government, many of the members of the
committee belonged to this party ; but the very strong cur-
rent of popular feeling in favour of the proceedings of congress, prevented that influence from interfering essentially
with the acts of the committee.

In the midst of this state of general excitement, the
British troops garrisoned in the city were ordered to join the
army in Boston. This order could easily have been prevented, and the troops made prisoners ; but the timidity of
the committee led them to suppose that such a step could
not be taken without the loss of a number of lives. They
therefore agreed to allow them to depart, with their arms

and accoutrements, without molestation. The troops accordingly marched from their barracks with the intention of embarking for Boston, about 10 o'clock in the forenoon of a fine pleasant day. There was a public-house in Water-street, near Beekman-slip, kept by a Mr. Jasper Drake : noted as a place of daily rendezvous for the warm friends of congress. It happened that Col. Willett, in company with a half dozen more of the same sentiments and spirit as himself, were together at this house, when word was brought to them, that the British troops were marching to the place of embarkation ; and that in addition to their own arms and accoutrements, they were also carrying off with them, on carts, chests filled with arms. Col. Willett and those at that time with him at Drake's, had been opposed to the permission granted the troops to depart at any rate ; and being further aroused, by the circumstance of their taking with them spare arms, not included in the grant of the committee, they suddenly determined to hazard the consequences of seizing these arms.

In pursuance of this bold and spirited determination, the company present set out by agreement on different routes through the city to alarm their friends. The route Col. Willett took led him to pass the Coffee House, where he stopped to give public notice of the course which was intended to be taken. He next proceeded through Water-street to the Exchange, which then stood at the lower end of Broad-street. At this place he observed the troops coming down the street; upon which he walked up to meet them. Coming close to the troops at the corner of Beaver-street, in Broad-street, and discovering several carts, loaded with chests of arms in front, under a small guard, Col. Willett, without a moment's hesitation, or waiting for any of his company to arrive, stopped the horse that was drawing the front cart-load of arms. An immediate halt in the whole line of march, of course, followed. This unexpected check brought the major of the regiment, who was for the time the commanding officer, in front, to inquire into the cause of the delay. Col. Willett had the horse by the head when he came up, and upon the major's enquiring into the meaning of the delay, he informed him that it was done with the intention of preventing the spare arms from being carried off, as the committee had not granted permission for the troops to take away with them any other than the usual arms and accoutrements. While Col. Willett was engaged in making this statement to the major, David Mathews, Esquire, who was at that time mayor of the city, came up, and accosted him in the following words : " I am surprised, Mr. Willett, that you will hazard the peace and endanger the lives of our citizens, when you know that the committee have directed that the troops shall be permitted to depart unmolested." It appears that Mr. Mathews was a tory, and a zealous supporter of the British government. This opposition therefore did not intimidate Col. Willett in the least, who at once replied, " that the committee had not authorized the troops to carry off any spare arms ; and that considering the bloody business which had taken place among our brethren in Massachusetts, whom they were bound by the ties of honor as well as interest to support, he deemed it his duty to prevent these arms from being used against them, by detaining them for the defence of his injured country."

At this juncture Mr. Governeur Morris came up, and to Col. Willett's great astonishment joined with the mayor in his opinion. This circumstance rather staggered Colonel Willett, as Mr. Morris was a whig himself, of very respectable connections; and though young, of brilliant talents.

The Colonel doubted whether all his zeal and enthusiasm would have been sufficient to support him, had it not been for the arrival at that critical moment of John Morin Scott, who was an influential member of the committee, and whose reputation for talent was not surpassed by that of any other individual in the city. He reached the spot, just as Colonel Willett was repeating to Mr. Morris the reason of his conduct, and exclaimed with a loud voice, "You are right, Willett : the committee have not given them permission to carry off any spare arms !"

The throng of people which had been all this while increasing, now pressed in on every side. Mr. Scott had no sooner declared his approbation of the course Colonel Willett had taken, when the Colonel turned the front cart to the right, and directed the carman to drive up Beaver-street : the other carts, loaded with arms, were ordered to follow.

Mr. Scott having suggested to Col. Willett the propriety of his addressing the troops, the Colonel leaped up on a cart, and invited such of the troops as felt a repugnance to shedding the blood of their countrymen, to quit their ranks, and come over to their side : assuring them in such case of protection. Upon this one of the soldiers, stepping out of the ranks, came over, and was received with three hearty huzzas. This soldier, together with the carts, five in number, were conducted with the continual huzzas of the citizens, through Beaver-street, and up Broadway as far as John-street.

There was in John-street a ball-alley and a large yard belonging to Mr. Abraham Van Wyck. Mr. Van Wyck was a good whig, who afterwards, when the British took the city, was made prisoner, and suffered a long and cruel captivity. In his yard the arms were deposited. These arms, and those taken possession of immediately after the account of the battle of Lexington reached the city, were used by the first troops raised in New-York under the orders of congress. The British troops meeting with no other impediment, agreeably to the order of the committee, marched to the wharf, and embarked amid the hisses of the citizens. It was Colonel Willett's opinion then and since, that it would have been as easy to have made prisoners of all the troops, as it was to seize upon these spare arms. But the thoughts of a compromise with the British government pervaded our councils and checked the adoption of spirited measures.

# CHAPTER IV.

—⊶⊕⊛⊕⊷—

DURING this period of general excitement, in the city of
New York, the spirit of the sons of liberty, as the firm and
warm friends of freedom were then denominated, struck
dismay and confusion among the adherents to the British
government. An enthusiastic emulation warmed the bosoms of the greater part of the citizens. It was owing to
this happy turn in the state of public feeling, not only in the
city, but throughout the colony of New York, that the recruiting of the troops for the defence of the country, which
soon after commenced, agreeably to the orders of congress,
was successfully executed.

The colony of New York was ordered to raise four regiments, each regiment to consist of ten companies. The
companies were directed to contain each seventy-two, rank
and file, four sergeants, a drum and fife, and to be placed
under the command of a captain and two lieutenants. Each
regiment was to be commanded by a colonel, a lieutenant-
colonel, and a major. Of the three regiments, the city of
New York was to furnish one.

Alexander McDougall, one of the prominent characters of
the day, and a man of considerable talents, was appointed
colonel of one of these regiments. The lieutenant-colonel

5

was Adolph. Ritzma, the son of a respectable minister of the Dutch congregation of the city of New York, who, it was understood, had been in the Dutch service in Europe. The major of the regiment was ———— Sedwitz, said to have been an officer in the service of Switzerland, his native country. Both these men, Ritzma and Sedwitz, proved to be, not only disqualified for the commands which they received, but traitors to the cause they professed to espouse.

After having, upon a variety of occasions shewn their incapacity, and having engaged in traitorous combinations, (for which one of them, the major, was apprehended and confined,) they both, finally, made their escape to the enemy. In the commencement of the revolution, the inexperience of the citizens led frequently to injudicious appointments. We were crowded with foreign impositions, and domestic ignorance. On this account, it is a greater cause of surprise, that the country should be able to support itself at all, than that it should meet with frequent disappointments and defeats; especially, when the almost total want of arms, ammunition, and money, is taken into consideration. The successful result of the war, under providence, is chiefly to be attributed to that happy enthusiasm, under the direction of the immortal Washington, which pervaded the great body of the people.

To the first New York regiment, commanded by Colonel McDougall, Colonel Willett was appointed the second captain. The first captain was Frederic Wisenfelts, a Prussian, who had been engaged in the Prussian service. In the war between Great Britain and France, he had been a lieutenant in the royal American regiment. Wisenfelts was a good officer, and had served with reputation during the greatest part of the war. So nice were his feelings of honour, as it respects the rank he held in the army, that he became deranged when the reform took place in the army, in the year 1780, by which his regiment became incorporated with another, the colonel of which was older than himself, and consequently assumed the command.

Colonel Willett received his appointment to the command of a company on the 28th of June, in the year 1775. He was in his thirty-fifth year. His health, his strength, the buoyancy of his spirits, his enthusiasm, were his principal qualifications. His company was one of the first that was recruited, and ready to take the field. On the 8th of August, he embarked on board of a sloop, with his company, for Albany, armed with those muskets which had been taken from the enemy. He arrived at Albany after a passage of four days. Three other companies arrived at the same time, under the command of colonel Ritzma. They were reviewed together by General Montgomery. After remaining a few days at Albany, they marched to Half-moon Point, from whence, after a half of a week, they proceeded to Ticonderoga, by the way of Skeenesborough. Here they were joined by a regiment of troops from Connecticut, commanded by Colonel Waterbury, and some other small detachments from New England.

On the twenty-ninth of August the troops, amounting to about one thousand men, under the command of General Montgomery, embarked on board batteaux, having an armed sloop and two other vessels of less force, to escort them over the Lake. On the 4th of September they landed on the Ile-aux-Noix, where they were joined by General Schuyler: upon whom, as the senior officer, the command then devolved. September the 6th, all the troops, with the exception of a detachment of one hundred men, who were left as a guard to the island, set out for St. John's, with the intention of investing and taking the fort at that place.

The troops having landed, had proceeded but a few hundred yards towards the fort, when they received a fire from an ambuscade of Indians. The fire was quickly returned; and the Indians soon fled. It was afterwards ascertained, that the loss of the Americans and that of the Indians was nearly equal. They had six killed and ten wounded.

At present, however, nothing of importance was attempted. The fort was found to be too well fortified to attempt to take it by storm. The troops remained under arms during the night; and the next day returned to the Ile-aux-Noix. Here they were daily reinforced by small detachments. On the tenth day of the month, one thousand troops, under the command of General Montgomery, proceeded again towards St. John's; and landed just at dusk, about two miles from the fort. From this place, Colonel Ritzma was detached with five hundred men to take post below the fort, in order to cut off the supply of the enemy. Captain Willett was with this detachment. As they were marching along the river, a few Indians from a log-house, which they had to pass, gave them a fire without doing any injury; two of the Indians were killed. This trifling impediment, owing to the conduct of Colonel Ritzma, balked the design of the expedition. General Montgomery, exceeddingly chagrined and mortified, returned the following day to Ile-aux-Noix.

Here they remained until the seventeenth : when having received a small supply of ammunition, two nine-pounders, and two small mortars ; and their force being augmented to near two thousand men, the army once more embarked under the command of General Montgomery, (General Schuyler on account of ill health having returned to Ticonderoga,) and landed late in the day at the place where the troops first disembarked. They passed the night without interruption. The next morning a detachment of five hundred men passed the fort, and took their station at the post which Colonel Ritzma had been formerly ordered to occupy. General Montgomery accompanied this detachment, and having succeeded in stationing it to his mind, returned to the place of landing. At this spot, ground was marked out for the troops to encamp. The distance from the fort being about a mile and a half, it was now regularly invested. In three or four days two batteries were erected: one between eight and nine hundred yards from the fort, on a point of land which overlooked it. On this battery two long iron nine-pounders were mounted. The other battery was erected about six hundred yards from the fort, in the woods ; on which two small mortars were placed.

During the greater part of the time that these works were going on, the enemy sent shot and shells. Four or five men were killed and wounded : but on account of their scanty supply of ammunition, the Americans were obliged to practice a rigid economy, so that little effect was produced by their fire : while the enemy, who were well furnished, returned ten shot for one.

About this time, General Montgomery was joined by a company of artillery, from New-York, under the command of Captain John Lamb. This company brought with them a small assortment of ordnance, stores, and some ammunition. A few days after they received a thirteen inch-mortar ; so that some shot and shells were fired every day. The fire of the enemy, however, annoyed even their camp ; while their elevated shot reached beyond it. Few were the means of the American northern army; but they made the most of them. After a sufficient trial, finding that but little was effected by their present position, a battery was erected on the opposite shore, nearer the fort, on the night of the sixth of October, consisting of three guns, which considerably annoyed the enemy.

At Chambly, twelve miles lower down the river, was a fort, garrisoned with upwards of one hundred and forty men, and commanded by Major Stopford. As soon as Gen. Montgomery was enabled, by re-inforcements, which were daily arriving, to lay siege to this place, its untenable situation soon brought on a capitulation, by which the garrison became prisoners of war. The stores taken at Chambly, and particularly the ammunition, were of great assistance.* This timely acquisition enabled the General to open a powerful battery against the fort at St. John's, from the north side. On the 3d of November the enemy were compelled to enter into articles of capitulation, surrendering themselves prisoners of war. The fort contained, besides the cannon mounted on it, a handsome train of artillery.

These successes deservedly procured General Montgomery the high encomiums of his country. Hard indeed was the work in which he was engaged. With awkward, undisciplined troops, difficult to control, to lie six weeks exposed to severe weather, on marshy, damp ground, without the means of making any serious impression upon the enemy, until he had supplied himself from their arsenals, required no common share of address, fortitude, and patience.

After the capture of Fort St. John's, Captain Willett was ordered with his company to escort the prisoners taken at Chambly, to Ticonderoga, so that he did not reach Montreal until the 22d of November. Having waited upon General Montgomery, he was directed to take command of Fort St. John's, where he remained until January; when the term for which his men were enlisted expiring, he was relieved,

---

* "A hundred and twenty-four barrels of powder were obtained on this occasion, besides a few pieces of cannon."

and again returned to Montreal. On the 18th of February he once more left that city for Albany, having the charge of some British officers and their families, who had been permitted, for their accommodation, to remain at Montreal until this time. He arrived at Albany towards the close of February, from whence, on the 1st of March, he set out on horseback for New York, which place he reached the evening of the fifth day of the month.

The war having now assumed a more severe and threatening aspect, and every circumstance conspiring to render it likely that it would be of long duration, the importance of a regular and permanent army appeared daily more and more apparent. Congress at length determined upon that measure; and issued orders at first for the enlistment of men for the whole war; but finding afterwards that the army recruited slowly for a term so indefinite, they ordered enlistments to be made for a term not less than three years.

According to this new arrangement, the different provinces were required to furnish eighty-eight battalions. Of this number, New York was to furnish four. Among the number of appointments that were made for the troops thus newly raised, Colonel Willett received, towards the end of November of this year, ('76,) that of Lieutenant Colonel to the third New York regiment. Along with this appointment, he received orders to repair to Fishkill, in order to recruit for the regiment. He was diligently employed during the winter in raising recruits, who, as they arrived, were drilled and clothed, as well as the situation of things would admit.

At the opening of spring, he was directed to march the troops to Fort Constitution, which garrison was placed under his command. The second and fourth New York regiments, which, with his, had rendezvoused during the winter at Fishkill, having previously marched to the lines, in West Chester County, and the fifth regiment having been sent to garrison Fort Montgomery, Colonel Willett's station, in the rear of the whole, left him a poor prospect of being soon called into active service. This interval of leisure was not lost; but was diligently employed in disciplining his troops. An unexpected opportunity of action, however, soon occurred.

On Sunday, the 22nd of March, just as the troops were parading for a field review, according to their usual custom every Sunday, Colonel Willett was informed, by express from General McDougall, (who commanded in this department, and was stationed at Peekskill, with the second and fourth New York regiments, and a detachment of Colonel Lamb's regiment of artillery,) that the enemy, having landed at that place, had caused him to retire to the high ground, at the entrance of the high lands. Colonel Willett was directed, after leaving a guard to take charge of the fort, to march the remainder of the troops to barracks, near where General McDougall had taken his quarters. Accordingly, the troops, with the exception of the guard, left to defend the fort, were immediately marched from the parade ground to the scene of action. They arrived at the barracks assigned them, about three o'clock, p. m. Colonel Willett reported himself, without delay, to the general, whom he found on the top of a hill, which overlooked all the country around Peekskill.

Just after Colonel Willett had made his report to the general, he saw the enemy set fire to a house near which they had posted a guard of about one hundred men. This small detachment of the enemy was stationed on a hill, six or seven hundred yards before their main body, while a considerable ravine lay between them. Conceiving it probable, that by a quick movement to the rear of this advanced body of the enemy, they might be attacked with advantage, and perhaps all of them taken, he proposed to General McDougall to make the experiment, with the troops which had arrived with him, provided the general, by a movement on Colonel Willett's left, would attract the attention of the enemy's main body. The proposal was objected to by General McDougall, who was of opinion that the enemy's force was too great for the hazard : he also expected considerable re-inforcements of the militia by the next morning, when he intended to advance upon the enemy. Colonel Willett, however, continuing to be a spectator of the depredations the enemy were committing, and feeling an earnest desire to check them, then requested permission to make the attack with his own troops. After a considerable time, and with much entreaty, General McDougall granted the request. But though Colonel Willett formed and marched his troops with the utmost celerity, yet, having two fences to cross, the sun was set before he could get sufficiently near the enemy, to make a charge with bayonets. In making this movement, they had received several fires from the enemy, but as soon as they rushed upon them with their bayonets, they fled. Their escape was aided by the darkness which followed.

Col. Willett was of the opinion, that if the attack had been made earlier, and followed up with resolution, there was but little doubt that the greater part of the enemy, the whole of whose force did not exceed six hundred men, might have been destroyed or taken. So great was their alarm, that in the course of two hours they were all on board of their shipping. What baggage the enemy had was left. It consisted only of a few blankets and cloaks.

6

Col. Willett had but two men killed, and four or five wounded. A blue camlet cloak, taken here, served afterwards to make the blue stripes of the flag which was hoisted during the siege of Fort Stanwix.*

The day after the hasty departure of the enemy from Peekskill, Col. Willett returned with his troops to Fort Constitution, where he remained until the 18th of May, employed in disciplining his recruits. Having been ordered to remove to Fort Stanwix, he set out for Albany with his regiment on board of three sloops, which place he reached the 21st. From Albany he went to Schenectady, and from thence to Fort Stanwix: but, owing to the number of loaded batteaux they had to take with them, they did not reach the Fort until the 29th.

---

* Appendix, No. 3.

# CHAPTER V.

—∞◦ƥ◦∞—

UPON Colonel Willett's arrival at Fort Stanwix, of which Colonel Gansevoort was the commandant, and himself the second in command, the fort was in a weak and untenable state. This fort, built where the village of Rome now stands, about half a mile from the Erie canal, was considered to be at that early period the principal key to the whole of the Mohawk country. It had been built, as we have seen, by General Stanwix, in the year 1758. It was a square fort,* with four bastions, surrounded by a ditch of considerable width and depth, with a covert way, and glacis around three of its angles; the other being sufficiently secured by low, marshy ground. In front of the gate there had been a drawbridge, covered by a salient angle, raised in front of it on the glacis. In the centre of the ditch, a row of perpendicular pickets had been erected, with rows of horizontal pickets fixed around the ramparts under the embrasures. But since the conclusion of the French war the fort had fallen into decay; the ditch was filled up, the pickets had rotted and fallen down.

---

* See in Appendix No. 4, a plate of the fort.

The engineer who had been employed to repair the fortifications was a French gentleman; but was wholly incom-
petent to his task. Instead of repairing the works after the
manner of their original construction, which could easily
have been done,—for though in a state of decay, the principal outlines of the old fort were still sufficiently visible,—
the engineer sent out large parties to procure logs from a
swamp. Having ordered them to be drawn near the fort,
he began to erect them in the covert way, and not in the
centre of the ditch, where they had formerly been placed.
After having with much labour procured the logs, it appeared that each log was seven feet longer than was necessary;
the logs being seventeen feet in length, when the pickets
that were to be made of them only required ten feet. This
blunder of the engineer, together with the general remiss-
ness he shewed at so critical a moment, led Col. Willett to
suggest to Col. Gansevoort the propriety of discharging him
from the office he filled. Col. Gansevoort, however, from
the circumstance that the engineer had been appointed
by the commander in chief of the northern department,
General Schuyler, to superintend the fortifications, was
reluctant to take this step.

The fortifications consequently continued to go on under
the superintendance of the engineer. The barracks were
repaired within the fort, and a large and commodious building, intended for this purpose, was erected a little beyond the
foot of the glacis. But all these works were of secondary
importance: indeed the barrack out of the fort at the foot
of the glacis, could be of no use in case of investment,
but rather an injury. And so it actually proved: for the
enemy set fire to this very building, at a time, when the wind
blowing fresh towards the fort, occasioned considerable in-
convenience to the garrison. In the meanwhile little was

done to strengthen the fort, though there was every reason to expect the instant arrival of the enemy.

The anxiety of Col. Willett, arising from a conviction of the incompetency of the engineer, in connection with the critical state of the fort, led him closely to inspect the progress of the fortifications. The engineer had begun to erect a salient angle to cover the gate, with two embrasures in it. He was also engaged in erecting pickets along the covert way. The pickets were placed about three feet from the parapet of the glacis. Two of them were framed together with cross pieces, and formed a kind of port-hole, which were intended to be placed opposite the embrasures. But it soon appeared from the manner in which the pickets were ranged, that the port-holes, formed of the pickets with cross pieces, would come opposite the neck of the embrasures. By this means the salient angle would be rendered wholly useless. Col. Willett at an early stage of the work, noticed the error, but thought it best to let the engineer take his own course, until the line of pickets should be carried to that part of the salient angle, where they would be opposite to the embrasures. When the engineer reached this part of his work, his ignorance would be without the least covering; and yet he never discovered his error, until the pickets were erected opposite the neck of the embrasures. Then for the first time he saw, that all his labour in erecting the salient angle had been in vain; and that it could not be used without first knocking away the neck of the embrasures. The case being stated to Col. Gansevoort, he directed Col. Willett to arrest the engineer, which was accordingly done. He was permitted to repair to head quarters; a letter at the same time being sent to Gen. Schuyler, assigning the reasons of the arrest.

It was not until some time in the month of July that this

step was taken. Information had already been received, that the enemy were advancing towards the garrison. Scouts of Indians, belonging to the enemy, had been frequently discovered in the vicinity of the fort. The approach of the enemy, and the prowling scouts of Indians, had rendered it necessary to issue orders, forbidding the garrison to go any distance from the fort, or to fire any guns, which had previously been allowed, pigeons being very abundant in the neighbouring woods.

Notwithstanding these orders, and the precautions that were taken, Captain Gregg, whose story is so familiar, and who belonged to Col. Willett's regiment, taking with him one of his corporals, proceeded about two miles from the fort; when, supposing his gun would not be heard, he commenced shooting pigeons; but being soon discovered by a scout from the enemy's Indians, both himself and his corporal were shot and tomahauked. Not far from the place where they were shot, two men were fishing, whose attention was attracted by the significant motions of a dog, who, running towards them, began to bark; he then ran back towards that part of the woods from whence he had issued, still continuing to bark, and looking back, as if entreating them to follow. The singular behaviour of this faithful and affectionate animal, induced the men to follow him, and by this means they were led to the spot, where Captain Gregg and the Corporal lay weltering in their gore. Alarmed by so unexpected and bloody a spectacle, they hurried to the fort, and, having told what they had seen, a party was immediately sent out to bring in the bodies of the unfortunate men. The corporal was dead, but signs of life were still seen in the captain. His case was, however, extremely critical; as he had received a shot which entered his side, ran along near the middle of the back, passing near the spinal bone, just beyond which it went out. He had also been struck with a tomahauk on the head, when he was scalped. Doctor Woodruff, the surgeon of the regiment, dressed his wounds; and the unremitting attention which he paid him, after a few days, removed the most alarming symptoms, so that hopes began to be entertained, that the captain would yet survive the terrible disaster. In about three weeks he was pronounced out of danger; and as the enemy were expected in the course of a fortnight, it was thought expedient that Captain Gregg, with the rest of the sick, and other ineffective persons, should be removed to Schenectady. The captain arrived safe at Schenectady, was restored to health, and remained in the service until the end of the war. He lived several years after the peace.

Captain Gregg recollected every circumstance of the transaction, and related it afterwards with great composure. It appears, that upon receiving the shot, he fell, and, seeing the Indian running towards him, he lay perfectly still, with the intention of leading the Indian to think he was dead; and when the Indian proceeded to scalp him, giving him at the same time a cut with his tomahauk on the upper part of his forehead, such was his fortitude through the whole of this trying scene, as to shew no signs of life. Shortly after the Indian left him, he looked around, and seeing the corporal lying at a short distance from him, he crawled up to him. He then took his watch out of his pocket to observe the hour of the day. Discovering after awhile that the corporal was dead, he laid his head on his body; and continued in that position, until he was taken up and conveyed to the fort.

The disaster of Captain Gregg, caused a greater degree of circumspection to be used in venturing at a distance from the fort, unguarded. Sunday, the 3rd of July, being a very warm, clear day, as Colonel Willett lay resting in his room about noon, three guns, fired in quick succession, gave him warning that there were Indians near. He ran to the gate of the fort, and on reaching the parapet of the glacis, saw a sentinel running towards the lower edge of it, and at a short distance from him a girl, also running, holding in her hand a small basket. On their coming nearer, he saw blood running down the breast of the little girl, who, as he afterwards learned, with two other girls, had been picking blackberries, not two hundred yards from the foot of the glacis, when they were fired at by the Indians. Upon going to the spot, Colonel Willett found the other two girls killed and scalped. One of the girls that was killed, was the daughter of a man who had served many years in the British artillery. He had been stationed as one of the guard at this post for several years. As he was considerably advanced in life, and infirm, he had received a discharge, with a recommendation to Chelsea hospital. But, as he had been indulged with the privilege of cultivating a piece of ground, and allowed the use of a small house to live in, he preferred remaining where he was, to returning to his native country, and enjoying the benefits to which his services entitled him. The girl who had made her escape, had been shot through the upper part of her shoulder: the wound proved to be slight, and she soon recovered.

A great degree of interest now began to be felt throughout the garrison. Indians were constantly hovering around them; and they soon became so numerous, that strong guards were sent out to protect the parties that left the fort. About the middle of July, one of these parties was attacked, several killed and wounded, and the officer who commanded taken prisoner. The enemy were instantly pursued, but without success. The condition of the fort rendered it improper to send out strong scouting parties, as every moment of time was required to prepare for defence.

The engineer having been dismissed, greater diligence than ever was necessary, to put the fort in a proper state of defence. Accordingly, officers as well as men exerted themselves with the utmost assiduity, and the work went on very rapidly. By the first day of August the wall around the whole of the fort was repaired; the parapets were nearly raised; embrasures made on three of the bastions; horizontal pickets fixed around the walls, and perpendicular pickets around the covert way. The gate and the bridge were also made secure, though the time had been too short to make any material alteration in the salient angle, so as to derive any benefit from it. The garrison had just finished laying the horizontal pickets at night, as the enemy invested the fort the next day; but at the time of the arrival of the enemy, none of the parapets had been completed. It was necessary, therefore, to finish these after the fort was regularly invested; and as the men engaged in work at them were unavoidably exposed, they became marks for the enemy's rifles, so that several of them were killed. The engineer had neglected to build a magazine, though he knew there was no secure place for the ammunition. The garrison, in order to remedy this difficulty, took the seven spare feet which were left of the pickets, in consequence of the mistake of the engineer as to their length, and having framed them, so as to form a square inclosure, the whole was placed within the body of one of the bastions, and being covered with earth, formed a safe deposit for the powder.

On the last day of July, advice was received that a number of batteaux loaded with ammunition and provisions, intended for the garrison, were on their way, under a guard of two hundred men. As the very safety of the fort de-

7

pended in a great measure upon their safe arrival, a detachment of one hundred men was sent out in order to assist them in case of need. These boats arrived about 5 o'clock, P. M., on the second day of August; and the stores were immediately conveyed into the fort. At the instant the last loads arrived, the enemy appeared on the edge of the wood near where the boats lay; and the captain who commanded them, remaining behind after all the rest had left, was taken prisoner.

The fort had never been supplied with a flag. The necessity of having one, had, upon the arrival of the enemy, taxed the invention of the garrison a little; and a decent one was soon contrived. The white stripes were cut out of ammunition shirts; the blue out of the camlet cloak taken from the enemy at Peekskill; while the red stripes were made of different pieces of stuff procured from one and another of the garrison.

The two hundred men who guarded the batteaux, were commanded by Lieut.-Colonel Mellon of Col. Weston's regiment. This reinforcement increased the number of the garrison to about seven hundred and fifty men, including officers and artificers. Upon examination, it appeared that they had provisions sufficient to support the garrison six weeks; but the ammunition was so scanty as to allow, for six weeks, only nine cannon to be fired per day. It was therefore necessary to use the cannon as little as possible. Of musket cartridges they had a sufficient quantity.

A flag came in from the enemy, the morning after their arrival. From this it was ascertained, that the troops investing the fort, were commanded by the British Colonel St. Leger, accompanied by Sir John Johnson. The flag left with the garrison one of Burgoyne's pompous declarations.

Very early on the morning of the 4th, a brisk fire from

rifles was commenced by the Indians, who, by concealing themselves behind the stumps of trees and other covers, considerably annoyed the men who were employed in raising the parapets. Several of them were wounded. Marksmen were immediately placed in different parts of the fortifications to return the fire as opportunities might offer. The greater part of the 5th, was spent by both parties in nearly the same manner, with the addition of a few shells thrown by the enemy from five-inch royals, several of which came within the fort, and some into the barracks. On the evening of this day, soon after it was dark, the Indians, who were at least one thousand in number, spread themselves through the woods, completely encircling the fort, and commenced a terrible yelling, which was continued at intervals the greater part of the night.

While the fort was thus invested, General Herkimer made an ineffectual attempt to relieve it. The general having collected with all possible despatch one thousand Tryon county militia, set out upon this expedition, having previously sent an express to Col. Gansevoort informing him of his intention. This express was brought by two men, who reached the fort in safety about 10 o'clock, on the morning of the 6th of August. The letter which the general sent, was dated the night before. Upon the receipt of the letter, agreeably to the directions of Gen. Herkimer, cannon were fired as a signal to let him know that the express he had sent had reached the fort in safety. Arrangements were immediately made to effect a diversion in favour of General Herkimer by a sally upon the enemy's camp. Accordingly, two hundred men were ordered on parade for this purpose, and placed by Colonel Gansevoort under the command of Col. Willett; but a heavy shower of rain coming up at that moment delayed the sally near an hour.

Gen. Herkimer, however, without waiting for the signal from the fort, which was to notify him that his express had been received, and that a sally would be made by the troops of the garrison to favour his approach, advanced prematurely upon the enemy, and without sufficiently reconnoitering the ground to guard against ambuscade and surprise. The general was a brave and resolute man : his troops were composed of Germans and Low Dutch ; and amongst them were the principal men of the county. They were enthusiastic in the cause they were endeavouring to support, impatient of delay, and under little subordination. They urged, and finally prevailed on the general to commence his march long before he could have expected the signal ; and of course before a diversion could be made in his favour from the fort. The enemy who were informed of his approach, had marched and taken possession of a commanding situation, about half way between their camp, and the place where he lay. The want of judgment in forming their line of march was another unfortunate circumstance for the general and his troops, in consequence of which, when they fell into the ambuscade laid for them, they were not in a condition to support each other. The militia in the rear (for the line of march was so scattered as to extend a mile in length) shewed but little courage : indeed many of them began early to make their escape.

Suddenly and unexpectedly attacked by the enemy, the general with a number of brave men formed themselves in a circle, and defended themselves with great gallantry. There were a variety of instances in which much personal courage was shown : in some cases attacks were made with tomahauks by the militia, as well as by the Indians, and with equal effect. The courage of the greater part of the militia was such as clearly shewed that if they had been sufficiently compact, and under such direction as to have been prepared to support each other, they would have been an overmatch for the enemy; but the loose manner in which they marched, and the want of precaution, produced such sudden confusion as could not be remedied. The action continued until the shower of rain commenced, when the enemy withdrew, and gave time for those brave men who remained on the field to collect their wounded ;* with whom they returned unmolested to the settlement.

As to the sally from the fort, it was completely successful. In addition to the two hundred men placed under Colonel Willett's command, mentioned before, fifty more were added to guard a light iron three-pounder, which increased his number to two hundred and fifty men. The cannon was mounted on a travelling carriage. With these troops, and this piece of mounted cannon, as soon as the rain ceased, Col. Willett lost not a moment in sallying forth from the gate of the fort. As the enemy's sentries were directly in sight of the fort, his movements were necessarily very rapid. The enemy's sentries were driven in, and their advanced guard attacked, before they had time to form their troops. Sir John Johnson, whose regiment was not over two hundred yards distant from the advance guard, and who himself, it being very warm, was in his tent with his coat off, had not time to put it on before his camp was forced. So sudden and rapid was the attack, that the enemy had not time to form so as to make any opposition to the torrent that

---

* Among the wounded was the gallant general himself, who received a shot in one of his legs, about six inches below the knee, which fractured the bone very badly. Col. Willett saw the wound dressed about two weeks after he received it. The leg itself was afterwards amputated. Col. Willett called to see the general soon after the operation. He was sitting up in his bed with a pipe in his mouth, smoking, and talking, in fine spirits. Early the next morning, however, he learned that the general had died in the night, having bled to death. Such was the unfortunate end of this brave man.

poured in upon them. Flight, therefore, was their only resource. Adjoining the camp of Sir John Johnson, was that of the Indians. This also was soon taken : so that a very few minutes put Col. Willett in possession of both these encampments. Sir John with his troops took to the river ; and the Indians fled into the woods. The troops under Col. Willett had fair firing at the enemy while they were crossing the river.

The quantity of camp equipage, clothing, blankets, and stores, which Colonel Willett found in the two camps, rendered it necessary to hasten a messenger to the fort, and have the waggons sent, seven of which were stored in the fort, with horses. These waggons were each three times loaded, while Colonel Willett and his men remained in the camps of the enemy. Among other articles, they found five British flags ; the baggage of Sir John Johnson, with all his papers ; the baggage of a number of other officers, with memoranda, journals, and orderly books, containing all the information which could be desired.

Colonel Willet, on returning to the fort, found Colonel St. Leger stationed, with such force as he could collect, opposite the landing, on the other side of the river, not more than sixty yards from the direction in which he was marching, with the intention of intercepting him. Colonel Willett's position, however, enabled him to form his troops so as to present him with a full fire in his front, while at the same time, he was enfiladed by the fire of a small field-piece ; and though Colonel St. Leger was sufficiently spirited in returning his fire, it was so wild, as to be altogether without effect. Colonel Willett returned in triumph to the fort, without having lost a single man.

Upon his return, the five flags, taken from the enemy, were hoisted on the flag-staff, under the continental flag ;

when all the troops in the garrison, having mounted the parapets, gave three as hearty cheers as, perhaps, were ever given by the same number of men.

Several prisoners were brought into the fort, among whom was a Mr. Singleton, a lieutenant of the light infantry company of Sir John Johnson's regiment. A few Indians and some troops were found dead in their camps, and, no doubt, several were killed in crossing the river. Upon the whole, the enterprize was successful, beyond Colonel Willett's most sanguine hopes. The loss of the enemy was, undoubtedly, great. Many of the articles taken from them were much wanted by the garrison. The happy result of this sally, appeared to inspire the garrison with an enthusiastic assurance of complete conquest over their enemies.*

The success with which the sortie from the fort was attended, added to the loss the enemy, and especially the Indians, had sustained in the action with General Herkimer, created considerable uneasiness in the enemy's camp. The afternoon of the next day, the beating of the chamade, and the appearance of a white flag, was followed with a request, that Colonel Butler, who commanded the Indians, with two other officers, might enter the fort, with a message to the commanding officer. Permission having been granted, they were conducted blindfolded into the fort, and received by Colonel Gansevoort in his dining-room. The windows of the room were shut, and candles lighted; a table also was spread,

---

* The following account of this sally, is taken from the British Annual Register, for 1777.

"On the day, and probably during the time of this engagement, (that is Herkimer's,) the garrison, having received intelligence of the approach of their friends, endeavoured to make a diversion in their favour, by a vigorous and well-conducted sally, under the direction of Colonel Willett, their second in command. Willett conducted his business with ability and spirit. He did considerable mischief in the camp, brought off some trophies, no inconsiderable spoil, some of which, consisted in articles that were greatly wanted, a few prisoners, and returned with little or no loss."

See Appendix, No. 5.

covered with crackers, cheese, and wine. Three chairs, placed at one end of the table, were occupied by Colonel Butler and the two other officers who had come with him : at the other end Colonel Gansevoort, Colonel Mellen, and Colonel Willett were seated. Seats were also placed around the table for as many officers as could be accommodated, while the rest of the room was nearly filled with the other officers of the garrison, indiscriminately ; it being desirable, that the officers in general should be witnesses to all that might take place. After passing round the wine, with a few common-place compliments, Major Ancrom, one of the messengers, with a very grave, stiff air, and a countenance full of importance, spoke, in nearly the following words : " I am directed by Colonel St. Leger, the officer who commands the army now investing the garrison, to inform the commandant, that the colonel has, with much difficulty, prevailed on the Indians to agree, that if the garrison, without further resistance, shall be delivered up, with the public stores belonging to it, to the investing army, the officers and soldiers shall have all their baggage and private property secured to them. And in order that the garrison may have a sufficient pledge to this effect, Colonel Butler accompanies me to assure them, that not a hair of the head of any one of them shall be hurt." (Here turning to Colonel Butler, he said, ' That, I think, was the expression they made use of, was it not ?'—to which the colonel answered, ' Yes.') " I am likewise directed to remind the commandant, that the defeat of General Herkimer must deprive the garrison of all hopes of relief, especially as General Burgoyne is now in Albany ; so that, sooner or later, the fort must fall into our hands. Colonel St. Leger, from an earnest desire to prevent further bloodshed, hopes these terms will not be refused ; as in this case, it will be out of his power to make them again. It was with great difficulty the

Indians consented to the present arrangement, as it will deprive them of that plunder which they always calculate upon, on similar occasions. Should, then, the present terms be rejected, it will be out of the power of the colonel to restrain the Indians, who are very numerous, and much exasperated, not only from plundering the property, but destroying the lives of, probably, the greater part of the garrison. Indeed the Indians are so exceedingly provoked, and mortified by the losses they have sustained, in the late actions, having had several of their favourite chiefs killed, that they threaten,—and the Colonel, if the present arrangements should not be entered into, will not be able to prevent them from executing their threats,—to march down the country, and destroy the settlement, with its inhabitants. In this case, not only men, but women and children, will experience the sad effects of their vengeance. These considerations, it is ardently hoped, will produce a proper effect, and induce the commandant, by complying with the terms now offered, to save himself from future regret, when it will be too late."

With the approbation of Colonel Gansevoort, Colonel Willett made the following reply. Looking the important major full in the face, he observed, " Do I understand you, Sir ? I think you say, that you come from a British colonel, who is commander of the army that invests this fort; and by your uniform, you appear to be an officer in the British service. You have made a long speech on the occasion of your visit, which, stript of all its superfluities, amounts to this, that you come from a British colonel, to the commandant of this garrison, to tell him, that if he does not deliver up the garrison into the hands of your Colonel, he will send his Indians to murder our women and children. You will please to reflect, sir, that their blood will be on your head, not on ours. We are doing our duty: this garrison is committed to our

8

charge, and we will take care of it. After you get out of it, you may turn round and look at its outside, but never expect to come in again, unless you come a prisoner. I consider the message you have brought, a degrading one for a British officer to send, and by no means reputable for a British officer to carry. For my own part, I declare, before I would consent to deliver this garrison to such a murdering set as your army, by your own account, consists of, I would suffer my body to be filled with splinters, and set on fire, as you know has at times been practised, by such hordes of women and children killers, as belong to your army."

The manner in which the message of Colonel St. Leger was received, together with the resolution of Colonel Gansevoort to come to no terms with the enemy, was re-echoed with applause by all the officers of the garrison who were present. Several of them pertinently remarked, that in their opinion, half the pains would not have been taken to induce them to surrender, if the enemy had not cause to fear that they should fail in their attempt.

Colonel St. Leger's deputation, seeing no likelihood of their terms being acceded to, asked permission for the surgeon, who accompanied their flag, to visit such of their wounded prisoners as had been taken in the sortie. This was granted; and while the British surgeon, in company with Mr. Woodruff, the surgeon of the garrison, was visiting the wounded, Major Ancrom proposed a cessation of arms for three days. As the garrison had more reason to fear the want of ammunition than provisions, this proposition was agreed to: soon after which the flag returned to their camp, and the troops of the garrison enjoyed a brief interval of tranquillity and ease.

The relief of the fort being still an object of the utmost importance, and no doubt remaining on the minds of any, but

that General Herkimer had been defeated, it was thought
advisable to make another effort for the purpose; and the
militia of Tryon county, having formerly expressed a particular attachment to Col. Willett, it was the general opinion that if he could shew himself among them, it might
have the effect of inspiriting them with fresh resolution, and
leading them a second time to exert themselves to raise the
siege. Influenced by these considerations Col. Willett agreed
to make the hazardous attempt to reach the settlements
down the river.

Accordingly, about 10 o'clock on the night of the 10th of
August, Col. Willett left the fort, accompanied by Major
Stockwell, whom he selected for this purpose, as he was a
good hunter, and was well acquainted with the Indian
method of travelling in the wilderness. They passed pri-
vately through the sally port of the fort, and proceeding
silently along the marsh, they reached the river, which they
crossed by crawling over a log unperceived by the enemy's
sentinels, who were not many yards from them. Having
thus happily succeeded in crossing the river without being
discovered, they advanced cautiously into a swampy wood,
where they soon found themselves so enveloped in darkness
as to be unable to keep a straight course. While in a state of
uncertainty as to the safest step for them to take, they were
alarmed by the barking of a dog, at no great distance from
them. Knowing that the Indians, after their camp had
been broken up on the other side of the river, had removed
it to this side, they thought it most advisable to remain
where they were, until they should have light sufficient to
direct their course. Placing themselves therefore against a
large tree, they stood perfectly quiet several hours. At length
perceiving the morning star, they again set out, but instead
of proceeding in a direct line to reach the settlement, they

took nearly a northerly direction, which after a few miles brought them again to the river. With the intention of concealing their route, in case their tracks should be discovered, they stepped in and out of the river several times, crossing occasionally to the opposite side, until reaching a spot where they could completely conceal their track by stepping on stones, they left the river, took a north course for a few hours, and then travelled east until night, without making a single stop. As it was necessary for them to be encumbered as little as possible, they had left the fort with no other weapon but a spear for each, eight feet in length, which was intended to serve as a staff as well as a weapon of defence. They had taken no baggage or blanket; and all the provision they had with them consisted of a few crackers and cheese, which they had put in their pockets, together with a quart canteen of spirits. Having halted for the night, they refreshed themselves with such provision as they had: after which, their situation being too perilous to think of kindling a fire, they lay down to sleep wrapped in each other's arms. Though it was then the height of summer, yet the night was so cold, as, together with hard travelling the day before, and sleeping on the ground without any covering, made them feel very stiff when they arose the next morning. ·Colonel Willett had so severe a rheumatic attack in one of his knees, as to cause a limp in his walk for several hours. Setting out once more, they directed their course farther to the south, and about 9 o'clock came to an opening in the woods, occasioned by a windfall. In this opening, among the fallen trees, they found a forest of raspberries and blackberries, quite ripe, which afforded them a most delicious and refreshing repast. Though the day was very warm, yet, deriving new vigour from their banquet of berries, they proceeded expeditiously towards the settlement, where they arrived at three o'clock, having travelled in this time about fifty miles.* On arriving at Fort Dayton, a small stockade fort at the German Flats, they received a hearty welcome from Colonel Weston, who was stationed there with his regiment. From Colonel Weston, Col. Willett obtained the agreeable intelligence that Gen. Learnard had been ordered by General Schuyler to march with his brigade of Massachusetts troops (which had been stationed on Van Schaick's Island, about ten miles above Albany,) to the relief of the fort.

Having rested that night at Fort Dayton, Col. Willett, still accompanied by Major Stockwell, set out on horseback early next morning to meet these troops, which they had the satisfaction of doing the very same night. Having been informed by General Learnard, that the troops intended for the relief of the fort, were to be commanded by General Arnold, who was at Albany, Colonel Willett proceeded next day to that place. Here he learned from General Arnold, that the first New York regiment was also on its march to join Learnard's brigade. The day following, Colonel Willett accompanied General Arnold to join the troops, and in two days arrived at Fort Dayton, where the whole force intended for the relief of the fort was assembled.

During Colonel Willett's absence from Fort Dayton, Lieutenant Walter Butler, with six or eight soldiers, and eight or ten Indians, had been taken prisoners. They had been surprised at the house of a Mr. Shoemaker, about two miles

---

* The British Annual Register for 1777, thus speaks of this enterprize.

"Colonel Willett afterwards (after the sally) undertook, in company with another officer, a much more perilous expedition. They passed by night through the besiegers' works, and in contempt of the danger and cruelty of the savages, made their way for fifty miles through pathless woods and unexplored morasses, in order to raise the country and bring relief to the fort. Such an action demands the praise even of an enemy."

from Fort Dayton, the evening previous to General Arnold's and Col. Willett's arrival at that place. Mr. Shoemaker was one of the King of England's justices of the peace; and being known by Mr. Butler to be disaffected to the congressional government, he had prevailed on him to assemble as many of the timid and disaffected inhabitants at his house as he could collect, with the intention of endeavouring to persuade them to join the army of Colonel St. Leger. Colonel Weston, having received information of what was going on, detached a party of soldiers, with orders to surround the house, and take the whole of them prisoners. This was promptly done; Mr. Butler being at the time in the midst of his harangue.

General Arnold having ordered a court martial, of which he appointed Colonel Willett judge advocate, in order to try Mr. Butler, as a spy from the enemy, the court found him guilty, and sentenced him to die; which sentence was approved of by General Arnold, and ordered to be put in execution the succeeding morning: but a number of officers belonging to the first New York regiment, petitioning to have him respited, the general granted their petition, and Butler was sent to Albany. He escaped from this place the winter following, and became afterwards a severe scourge to the inhabitants of these frontiers.

Shortly after this, the news of the approach of General Arnold, to relieve the fort, having reached the enemy, the Indians being already extremely disaffected, in conseqence of the ill success of the siege, and Colonel St. Leger, finding that the mulish obstinacy, as he termed it, in a letter written to General Burgoyne, of the garrison, could not readily be overcome, on the 22nd of August the siege was suddenly abandoned, after it had been carried on twenty days.

Throughout the whole of the siege, Colonel St. Leger,

certainly, made every effort in his power to render it successful. Having sent after Colonel Willett's departure, to Colonel Gansevoort, a written summons to surrender, which he found as unavailing as his message by Major Ancrom, he commenced approaching by sap, and had formed two parallels, the second of which brought him near the edge of the glacis, but the fire of the musketry from the covert way, rendered his further progress very difficult ; besides, his ordnance was not sufficiently heavy to make any impression from the battery which he had erected. The only way in which he could annoy the garrison, was with his shells, and this was so trifling, as to afford him but a poor prospect of success. It appears, that he made large calculations upon intimidating the garrison with threats ; and, perhaps, his expectations were the more sanguine, as Ticonderoga had been but a little time before abandoned, upon the approach of General Burgoyne.

The unexpected and hasty retreat of Colonel St. Leger, and his host of Indians, accompanied by Sir John Johnson, whose influence among the settlers along the Mohawk river, it was supposed, would procure considerable reinforcements, defeated all the calculations that had been made in the event of the success of St. Leger, which was hardly doubted. Great indeed was the disappointment and mortification, when, instead of Colonel St. Leger taking the fort, and, by this means, obtaining possession of the Mohawk country, as well as effecting a junction with General Burgoyne, he was obliged to retreat, wholly baffled in all his designs.*

---

* "Nothing," says the British Annual Register, " could have been more untoward in the present situation of affairs, than the unfortunate issue of this expedition. The Americans represented this and the affair at Bennington, as great and glorious victories. Nothing could exceed their exultation and confidence. Gansevoort and Willett, with General Starke and Colonel Warner, who had commanded at Bennington, were ranked among those who were considered as the saviours of their country."

After the retreat of the enemy, Colonel Willett passed several months in comparative inactivity. Colonel Gansevoort, having gone to Albany, the command of the fort devolved on him. He improved this interval, in completing the works, and disciplining the troops. Toward the last of September, Colonel Gansevoort, having returned to the fort, Colonel Willett set out to visit his family at Fishkill, where he arrived, the very day on which Fort Montgomery was taken. During this visit he was not inactive, but assisted in the defence of that part of the country against the enemy, who, having obtained the entire possession of the Hudson river, threatened the inhabitants along its banks, at every point. After this, he visited the grand army, under the immediate command of General Washington, which he found encamped at White Marsh, about twelve miles from Philadelphia. It was late in January before he returned to the fort, where he continued until the following June

# CHAPTER VI.

—◦◦◦◦◦—

## BATTLE OF MONMOUTH.

WEARIED with the inactive life he led, and seeing no prospect of more brilliant service in that remote section at that period, Colonel Willett once more, with the approbation of Colonel Gansevoort, set out to visit the commander-in-chief, with the view of endeavouring to have the regiment relieved, and of joining the main army; objects which he was extremely desirous of effecting. At Peekskill he found Gen. Gates; and happened to be at his quarters on the night of the 21st of June, when an express from Gen. Washington brought advice of the evacuation of Philadelphia by the enemy. Gen. Gates, having suggested his intention of sending a confidential messenger to Gen. Washington, with a statement of the force and magazines under his command, which, as the army under Washington would probably move that way, it was necessary he should be well acquainted with, Colonel Willett was pleased with the opportunity of offering his services on that occasion. Having accordingly been furnished with a fresh horse, which the quarter-master was ordered to procure for the purpose, he crossed the river the next morning, and arrived at head-quarters the evening of the same day. Having finished his business with the commander-in-chief, he obtained from him permission to

9

remain with the army. On Wednesday the 23d of June, being the morning after his arrival, he was informed that a detachment of light troops under the command of General Scott of Virginia, was ordered to march towards the enemy, with the intention of harassing them on their retreat. Having obtained an introduction to General Scott, Colonel Willett offered himself as a volunteer aid, and his offer being cordially accepted, he had the satisfaction of remaining with him until after the battle of Monmouth, which took place the Sunday following.

General Scott's detachment of light troops marched the first day to within a few miles of the enemy's rear: in the evening of the same day, it was joined by the Jersey brigade. Early the next morning they got upon the enemy's track, which they followed; but as their columns were kept close, and their line of march was compact, no opportunity of an advantageous attack presented itself. A few prisoners and deserters were all that fell into their hands. As the weather was very warm, and the country through which they passed barren and sandy, the troops suffered for want of water: the more so as the enemy had taken care to fill up the wells. In the evening General Scott was re-inforced with upwards of one thousand men under General Wayne; and the command of the whole detachment was put under the Marquis De La Fayette.

Early on the morning of the 27th, an attempt was made to impede the march of the enemy by an attack upon their rear; but it was ineffectual: and they continued their route to Monmouth Court-House. In the course of the day the detachment was increased to five thousand; and the command conferred on General Lee. Early on Sunday morning, being the 28th of June, a smart fire was commenced, just as the enemy began to march. This attack became so serious that the enemy found it necessary to halt their line, and turn the whole of their force upon us. The light infantry to which Colonel Willett was attached were formed on the edge of the wood, when the Marquis De La Fayette galloping up to them, told them that the British grenadiers were advancing to gain their right; and ordered them to march with a quick step to oppose them. This order was obeyed with alacrity: but as the enemy had halted beyond a marshy piece of gound; and by their last movement the light infantry had become separated from the rest of the troops, General Scott took an advantageous position, which he had just gained, when he was ordered to retire. General Scott conceiving that the order would be countermanded, if General Lee were once made acquainted with the excellence of his position, sent Colonel Willett to give him a particular account of its advantages in case the enemy should advance to attack them. Before Colonel Willett could find the general, he observed that all the troops were retiring: when near the Court-House, he fell in with General Wayne, and at the same time General Scott rode up and informed him that he had received a second order, and that the troops had of course left their position, and were retiring. Both these gentlemen expressed great mortification at the measures adopted; and pointed out several important advantages which might be gained by waiting the attack of the enemy, who were then advancing pretty rapidly towards them.

While Colonel Willett, with Generals Scott and Wayne, were conversing together, they discovered General Lee, for the first time, since the troops commenced retreating, on a pretty conspicuous piece of ground, and, anxious to learn the cause of the retreat, rode fast towards him. It appears, that some person had already suggested to the general some doubts as to the propriety of the movements the troops were making; for just as Colonel Willett got within reach of hearing, the first words that struck his ears, from General Lee, were, "It does not signify,—the enemy have too much cavalry for us."

The enemy, perceiving that a retreat had commenced, moved forward more rapidly. The fire from their artillery had become brisk.

The enemy had brought their cavalry in front: and the only clever thing Colonel Willett witnessed, on the part of General Lee, was, that on observing the cavalry advancing, he ordered some troops to a good position, to check them; when, calling his dog, he left the spot where he was, and joined the troops he had stationed to oppose the enemy's cavalry. These, advancing on a canter, received so severe a fire, as completely broke and dispersed them. Here a horse was to be seen galloping away without its rider. and there a horseman rising from the dust.

A brisk fire of musketry, as well as artillery, had now commenced in different parts of the line. The weather was extremely warm. Some of the troops, especially such as had charge of field-pieces, were obliged to break their columns, in order to avoid a marsh, across which they could not carry the artillery. This was the case with some of General Scott's detachment of light infantry, who had charge of two field-pieces. This being observed by the enemy, they detached a regiment of Highlanders, to attack General Scott's detachment. The Highlanders advanced briskly across an orchard to the attack, but were received by a well-directed fire, which killed upwards of thirty of them in a few minutes.

By this time General Washington had arrived on the field; and put a stop to the retrograde movement: such a line was formed as effectually checked the advance of the enemy. Two formidable lines were formed, in front of each other, to a considerable extent. The fire of artillery from both lines was severe, and not without execution. It was doubtful, on which side the artillery was best served; but, in every instance, where our musketry was opposed to the enemy's, the advantage was, evidently, on our side.

General Washington, who never to Colonel Willett appeared so great as he did on that day,* (though to him, he always appeared greater than any body else,) was mounted on a fine large sorrel horse : he had a spy-glass in his hand, and from a commanding situation, within the line of the enemy's fire, he seemed to observe and know everything. Firmness, composure, and dignity sat on his brow. His presence inspired universal ardour along the line ; and, in the poetical description of Mr. Addison,

"He taught the doubtful battle where to rage."

General Washington's situation within the line of fire, with a number of officers about him, appeared to attract the attention of the enemy, so as to induce them to direct their fire on that more than any other part of the line. Colonel Willett happened to be near him, when this was evidently the case, and directed one of his aides to ride round among the officers and request them to withdraw, as they offered a mark for the enemy's fire, Upon this intimation a number of them withdrew ; and Colonel Willett then retired to that

---

*The appearance of General Washington, says Colonel Willett, was such, as to excite admiration and respect. I recollect feeling these sentiments the first time I ever saw him, which was the year after the memorable defeat of General Braddock. He was then only twenty-three years of age. His manly, sedate countenance, and deportment, together with the fineness of his person, forcibly attracted attention and respect, even in those his youthful days. Nineteen years had elapsed, from that period to the time of my seeing him again, which was a few days after he was appointed to command the American army. His greatness appeared to have increased with his years. His noble countenance displayed the greatness of his mind ; and his whole demeanour was calculated to command veneration. I have seen him in a variety of situations, and none in which he did not appear great : but never did I see him when he exhibited such greatness as on this day.

part of the line where the light infantry was formed. He had been there but a few minutes, when two gentlemen riding slowly along, he heard one of them exclaim, "Poor Lee." As General Lee was near General Washington at the time Colonel Willett left the spot where he was, on hearing the exclamation of, "Poor Lee," he concluded he was killed; and, turning to the person who made the exclamation, enquired if Lee was shot; to which he replied, "No: but he is a great deal worse off,—for the general has given him a most severe reprimand, and ordered him to English Town, (which was four miles in the rear,) with orders to collect such scattered troops as he might find, and assemble them at that place."

In the meanwhile, by a well-timed order, General Green and Lord Stirling took possession of commanding ground, from whence a heavy fire so enfiladed the enemy's line, as to compel them to retreat. The position they left was instantly occupied by the American troops; and so hot a fire poured in upon the enemy, as compelled them to retreat. The late hour of the day necessarily prevented any further operations: except placing such part of the army as had experienced the least fatigue, in such positions, as would enable them to commence another attack early the next morning. But this was prevented, by the retreat of the enemy in the night, leaving their wounded behind them.* They had taken the road towards Sandy Hook; and when it was discovered they had retreated, were so far ahead, as not to render it advisable to pursue them with the army. Some light troops were ordered to follow at a distance, with a view of picking up any deserters, or stragglers, from the enemy, while the

---

* As General Washington had ordered Colonel Morgan, with his rifle corps, which was reinforced by some other troops, by a circuitous march to attack the enemy's baggage, the victory would have been much more complete, if the attack had not been prevented by the retrograde movement of General Lee.

main army filed off towards Brunswick : but, learning that the enemy had landed at New York, they marched towards the Hudson, which they crossed at Stony Point.

The remainder of the campaign, of the year '78, after the battle of Monmouth, Colonel Willett spent with the main army, which encamped in West Chester county.

The campaign of '79 he spent with General Sullivan, on the western expedition against the hostile Indians, destroying their crops and towns.

In the hard winter of '79, '80, while the main army was in winter quarters, four miles from Morris Town, in the woods, Colonel Willett received orders to cross over to Staten Island, to attack Colonel Van Bushkirk. With five hunded men, and one field-piece, he crossed at night, upon the ice ; and waited until day-light to commence the attack. Day having broke, he rode forward to reconnoitre. He soon found that the house, occupied by Van Bushkirk, was closed, windows and doors being shut. Seeing a woman standing in the door of a house opposite, he enquired of her what had become of Bushkirk. She said, he was in the house. It appears, however, that having obtained information of the intended attack, he had departed, with such precipitancy, as to leave behind all his stores. Colonel Willett loaded seventeen waggons with stores, consisting of sugar, butter, gin, &c., which came very seasonably for the army.

The same winter he made an expedition to Powle's Hook, and, having taken a redoubt, drove away all the English cattle.

In the year '80, Colonel Willett commanded the 5th New York regiment, which was connected with the grand army. Nothing material, however, transpired this year, so far as he was concerned.

# CHAPTER VII.

—⊷⊶⊙⊷⊶—

## MOHAWK CAMPAIGNS.

Towards the close of the year '80, the reform took place which reduced the five New York regiments to two. Upon this change, Col. Willett was ordered to take command of all the levies, militia, and state troops, that might be raised to protect the north-west frontiers of the State of New York, in which command he continued to the end of the war.

It was at the earnest solicitation of Governor Clinton, that he was induced to undertake the defence of this important frontier. He quitted the main army with extreme reluctance, unwilling to deprive himself of the opportunity of serving his country in that more public scene of action. But yielding to the repeated requests of governor Clinton, who in his letter to him on this subject, expressed his belief, that he could be of essential service to the State in that exposed section of it ; the more so, to use the governor's own language, "as he was informed that the inhabitants of Tryon county placed the highest confidence in his zeal and military abilities ;" he at last consented to the governor's proposition. Having once engaged in this arduous service, sympathizing in the sufferings of the inhabitants of that frontier, anxious to inflict upon the Indians, and especially upon the tories, (whom Governor Clinton in one of his letters to him, styles "cruel monsters worse than savages,") as being the chief instigators, and the most barbarous actors in the cruelties and devastations that were committed along this extended frontier, he entered upon the arduous duties of the campaign with diligence and alacrity.

The following letters of Col. Willett to General Washington and Governor Clinton, will give an account of the condition of the county, both before and at the time of his arrival there : the mode of defence against the savages that was adopted by the inhabitants ; and the measures he himself took for their security.

*German Flatts, Fort Herkimer, July 6th,* 1781.

Sir,—I am in this county* by order of Governor Clinton. Among other particulars in the instructions I have received from him, are the following. "For a variety of reasons, I conceive it will conduce most to the good of the service that you should take post yourself in Tryon county. In the distribution of the troops, you are to have regard to the aid to be derived from the continental troops, and militia : to whom I will give such orders as will enable you to avail yourself of their aid."

In consequence of these orders, and in expectation of the legislatures making provision to execute a plan, of which I had given a sketch to Governor Clinton, I am at present on these frontiers. Impelled by the situation of things in these parts, I beg leave to lay before your Excellency a short description of this country, with its present condition.

It is a country of the most luxuriant soil. Not only the lands along the river are exceedingly rich, but the back

---

* Tryon county, embracing at that time all that part of the State of New York, west of the county of Albany.

lands are also of the first quality. This tract of country exceeds any I passed through in our march upon the western expedition under General Sullivan. Most of the settlements lie along, or not far back from the Mohawk river. At the commencement of the present war, both sides of the river, from Schenectady to Germantown, which is seventy miles, the settlements were considerably thick; and every thing had the appearance of ease and plenty. There were besides several valuable farms, extending fifteen miles higher up the river than Germantown. Germantown, however, is the last place where any number of families had fixed themselves together. At the beginning of the war the militia of the county did not amount to less than two thousand five hundred men. In such a country, blessed with so fine a soil, lying along a delightful river, which affords an easy transportation of the produce to a valuable market, with a climate exceeded by none, one would have expected a consequent increase of population. But this was retarded by means which you are undoubtedly acquainted with. The obstructions to its future growth and prosperity, will, I hope, in a little time be removed; and this part of the world, which is, perhaps, one of the first places on this continent, be surpassed by none. Flourish it must. Nothing but the hand of tyranny can prevent it much longer from becoming the garden of America.

The place from which I now write, is, at present, the advance settlement up the river, and lies sixty-three miles from Schenectady. This strip, sixty miles in length, is liable to Indian incursions, on both sides of the river. This the inhabitants have frequently experienced; and so severe has been their experience, that, out of two thousand five hundred upon the militia rolls, at the commencement of the war, at present, the whole number of classible* inhabitants does not amount to one thousand two hundred. Of classible inhabitants, (that is, of those who were liable to be assessed to pay taxes, in order to raise men for the public service,) there being not twelve hundred, the number liable to be called upon to do military duty, will hardly exceed eight hundred; so that there is a reduction in the county of at least two thirds, since the commencement of the war.

To account for this large reduction, I do not think I am wild in my calculations, when I say, that one third of them have been killed, or carried captive by the enemy; one third have removed into the interior parts of the country; and one third deserted to the enemy. The present distressed situation of the inhabitants, is such, as to demand sympathy, from the most unfeeling heart. Each neighbourhood has erected for itself a fortification. Within these forts, the inhabitants have in general taken up their residence. Each fort contains from ten, to upwards of fifty families. There are twenty-four of these fortifications within the county. Pitiable, indeed, is the case of a people, thus situated. But, wretched as their situation is, such is the state of the country; and in such a condition are the people who inhabit it. But, notwithstanding their deplorable situation, should they be fortunate enough to preserve the grain they at present have in the ground, they will have an immense quantity more than will be sufficient for their own consumption.

To protect this country, as much as possible, is our present business; and this is the point, to which I now wish to call your Excellency's attention. By withdrawing the regular

---

* By a law of the State of New York, every male person, not being a slave, who was above sixteen years of age, was to be numbered into classes. Individuals of each class, were, respectively, to pay as much towards raising men for the public service, as they were assessed, by persons appointed for that service.

troops, the county is, undoubtedly, much weakened. At this time, I have not, in the whole county, more than two hundred and fifty men, exclusive of the militia. Some reinforcements, Governor Clinton writes me word, are coming from the eastward. Part of these, we may hope, will come this way; and, by others being sent to the northward, I flatter myself, I shall be able to withdraw those levies, which have been placed under my command, which are, at present, that way.

I heartily wish to have as much force as possible, to assist in the preservation of a people, whose sufferings have, already, been so exceeding great. But, be the force larger or smaller, I can only promise to do everything in my power, for the relief of a people, of whom I had some knowledge in their more prosperous days; and am now acquainted with in the time of their deep distress: a people, whose case I most sincerely commiserate. At the same time, I think it my duty to inform your Excellency, that, after withdrawing the two regular regiments from these parts, I expect to have the command of all the troops that may be ordered into this county for its common defence. This is what Governor Clinton told me would be the case. Should the legislature make such further provision, for the defence of the county, as I have requested, notwithstanding its present deplorable situation, I shall hope to have the state of things much more respectable than hitherto it has been. Nor shall I exceed my hopes, if, in the course of less than twelve months, I shall be able to convince the enemy, that they are not without their vulnerable quarters, in these parts.

Since I have been in this part of the country, I have been endeavouring to put matters in some kind of regulation. With the approbation of the governor I have fixed my quarters at Canajoharie, on account of its central position.

And my intention is to manage business so as to have an opportunity of acquainting myself as well as possible with every officer and soldier I may have in charge. In order the better to do this, I propose, as far as I can make it any way convenient, to guard the different posts by detachments, to be relieved as the nature of the case will admit. And as the relieved troops will always return to Fort Rensselaer, where my quarters will be, I shall have an opportunity of seeing them all in turn. Having troops constantly marching backwards and forwards through the country, and frequently changing their route, will answer several purposes, such as will easily be perceived by you, sir, without my mentioning them. This is not the only way by which I expect to become particularly acquainted with the troops and their situation. I intend occasionally to visit every part of the country, as well to rectify such mistakes as are common among the kind of troops I have at present in charge, as to enable me to observe the condition of the militia, upon whose aid I shall be under the necessity of placing considerable reliance.

In order to shew that I have some reason to place dependence upon the militia, I shall first mention a transaction that took place a few nights ago at Canajoharie. An account was sent me at one o'clock in the morning, that about fifty Indians and tories were in the neighbourhood of a place six miles off. Having with me at the fort no more regular troops than were sufficient to guard it, I sent for a captain of the militia ; and in less than an hour he was out with seventy men in search of the enemy. In short, they are a people, who, having experienced no inconsiderable portion of British barbarism, are become keen for revenge, and appear properly determined.

It is with regret I trespass upon your time in this manner: but I am desirous of giving you as good a sketch as I can of the situation of this country. It is easy for you to perceive that the strength we now have this way is inadequate to the fortress intended to be erected at this place by Major Villa...., the engineer, who was ordered here for the purpose of fortifying this place. Nor did I see the great necessity of such works being erected here. I humbly conceive that some small improvements to the works we already have, will answer our present purpose. And I am pretty clear it will be all that we shall be able to accomplish.

If it should meet with your approbation, I should be glad to make such a disposition of the cannon and other ordnance stores, as may appear most secure, and best calculated to protect the country. For to me it is clear, that the way to protect these parts is, in case the enemy should again appear this way with any thing of force, to collect all the strength we can get to a point, and endeavour to beat them in the field, and not attempt to defend any one particular spot: for such is the exposed state of the country, that the enemy can make incursions in almost any quarter. Beside this, it is not their policy or custom to halt to invest any particular place. It is therefore my opinion, that by joining our whole force together, and not by defending any one post, we are to endeavour to protect these frontiers: whilst these small stockade forts, and block houses, which the inhabitants themselves have built, are in general sufficient to cover them against such parties of Indians and tories as usually make this way.

I should count myself happy in having your sentiments upon this subject. At present I have at this place about one hundred men: nor is it possible without calling on the inhabitants below, to afford this place more men until I receive some reinforcements. I need not say to you, sir, that nothing can be done towards erecting the new fort, with the men I now have. I shall, therefore, only endeavour to repair the works already at this place, until I shall receive further orders

  I have the honour to be with the greatest sincerity
    your Excellency's most obedient
      and humble servant,
        MARINUS WILLETT.

*To His Excellency, Gen. Washington,*

---

*German Flatts, July 6tn, 1781.*

SIR,—At present I am at this place, with one hundred and twenty of the levies, including officers; and captain Moody's company of artillery, which is but twenty strong. The total of all the levies in this county beside is ninety-six. A very insufficient number indeed to perform such business as is expected from us. I am crowded with applications for guards, and have nothing to guard with. I will, however, do my best, and have no doubt, you will pay as much attention to our situation as you can.

That part of my regiment of levies not with me at this place, is stationed as follows. At Schoharie I have placed a little over twenty men : Kaatskill about the same number, unless they have received recruits from Dutchess County, where I ordered them to send officers for that purpose. Captain White has his company still at Ballstown, except a few left with the commissioners of Albany, which I have ordered to join him. This whole company consists of about thirty men. Captain Whelp's company is ordered this way from Saratoga, where the companies of Captains Gray and Dunham still remain. I shall endeavour to make some alterations, but am at a loss, with the very few men we have, to know how. I shall be glad to have your sentiments on this matter as soon as possible. I confess myself not a little disappointed in having such a trifling force for such extensive business as I have upon my hands; and also that nothing is done to enable me to avail myself of the aid of the militia. The prospect of a suffering country hurts me. Upon my own account I am not uneasy. Every thing I can do shall be done ; and more cannot be looked for. If it is, a reflection that I have done my duty, must fix my own tranquillity.

I am your Excellency's most obedient<br>and very humble servant,<br>MARINUS WILLETT.

*To His Excellency, Gov. Clinton.*

In the preceding campaign of 1780, the defence of the Mohawk country had been committed to Colonels Malcomb, Dubois and Brown, aided by three regiments of levies. During that year the enemy made an incursion in that quarter ; and marching deliberately through the country, laid it waste on both sides of the river. The only opposition they met with in this cruel incursion, was from Col. Brown, who was himself slain. This disastrous campaign, in connection with other losses and attacks, had so completely disheartened the inhabitants that few remained upon their farms.

In the beginning of July, '81, Col. Willett arrived at Fort Rensselaer, his head quarters, and relieved Colonel Courtland, who had been stationed in this quarter with a regiment of continental troops. Soon after his arrival, he received advice that the enemy in considerable force were destroying the settlements at Corey's Town, which lay about eleven miles to the south-east of where he was. The steps

Colonel Willett took to repel this incursion will be seen in the following letter to Governor Clinton.

*Fort Rensselaer, 1st July,* **1781.**

Sir,—In my letter of yesterday, I informed your Excellency, that, while I was writing, several smokes were discovered to the south-east; and that they were supposed to be produced by the enemy setting fire to Corey's Town. I had, early in the morning, detached thirty-five men of the levies, under the command of Capt. Gross, to Thurlough, but, upon the discovery of the smoke, I sent an express to Capt. Gross, to try to find out the track of the enemy. At the same time that the express was sent off to Captain Gross, I detached Captain McKain, with sixteen levies, with directions to collect as many of the militia as he could, and move towards Corey's Town. Notwithstanding this settlement was eleven miles from this place, Captain McKain was in time to assist in saving some of the buildings, by quenching the fire. In the mean time, I was endeavouring to collect as many of the militia as I could, in order to join with the few levies I had, to go in pursuit of the enemy. It was dusk before I could get ready to march; and when I did march, the whole of my force, after being joined by the detachment of Captains McKain and Gross, was only one hundred and seventy strong. I had been so fortunate, as to discover, not only the track of the enemy, but the place where they had encamped the same day; and had reason to think, that they would return there again, and, probably, that night. This determined me to march directly to the place of their encampment. Notwithstanding it was reported that the enemy were numerous, and the distance to the encampment eighteen miles, still I conceived it possible to arrive there before day, and, perhaps, surprise the enemy asleep in their encampment.

This I should have accomplished, had it not been for the thickness of the woods, and the guide losing his way, for a considerable time, in the dark. In consequence of this delay, it was near six o'clock in the morning before our arrival, so that the enemy discovered our approach in time to prepare for our reception. They had left their camp, and taken other and better ground, so that we had to prepare for the attack under some disadvantages. The enemy, however, who were nearly of the same number with us, did not wait for us to begin the attack, but, with great appearance of determination, by their yelling and shouts, advanced, and began the fire. This was the fury of Indians, and nothing else; for upon the huzzas and advance of the front line, they soon gave way. At the same instant, another attack of the same kind was made upon our right, and would have been more injurious to us, had it not been for our reserve under the command of Captain McKain, who returned the attack with such spirit, that the enemy, dispersing in small parties, soon sought safety in flight."

This battle lasted an hour and a half. The enemy's force consisted of about two hundred. Our loss, in killed, was five; missing and wounded, nine. The enemy's loss was supposed to be not less than forty, as near that number were found dead, on and near the place of action.

In this action, Captain McKain, a brave, and very valuable officer, received a wound, of which he died, before he got to Fort Rensselaer, where he was buried. He had a son with him, a fine lad, who was likewise wounded, but recovered.*

* See in Appendix, No. 6, the resolution of the Common Council of the city of Albany, presenting Colonel Willett with the freedom of the city, for this victory. See, also, in Appendix, No. 5, the resolution of Congress, presenting Colonel Willett with a sword, in commemoration of the sortie from Fort Stanwix.

In consequence of the happy effects of this action, but little trouble was experienced from the enemy through the remainder of the summer. They were sometimes discovered, but in no considerable bodies; and being always pursued, they fled, without doing much injury. In the afternoon of the 24th of October, however, word was brought, that the enemy had appeared, in considerable force, at Warrensbush, upwards of twenty miles from Fort Rensselaer. No time was lost. Collecting all the force that could be mustered, and sending orders, at the same time, for the levies and militia, in the contiguous posts and settlements, to follow, Colonel Willett set out that very afternoon, marched all night, and on his arrival in the morning at Fort Hunter, learned that the enemy had crossed the river, and, at this time, were at Johnstown. A regular British soldier, who, by fatigue, had been prevented from crossing the river with the troops, having fallen into the hands of the inhabitants, they ascertained that the enemy's force was upwards of eight hundred good troops, and one hundred and twenty Indians, commanded by Majors Ross and Butler. As the water at Fort Hunter was too deep to ford, and the troops had to pass in batteaux, it was in the afternoon before all the troops had crossed the river. As soon as the passage of the river was effected, they proceeded to march, by sections, towards Johnstown. On counting the sections, it was found, that there were one hundred and four, making four hundred and sixteen men. This was only about half the number of the enemy's troops, without including the Indians. When within two miles of Johnstown, Colonel Willett was informed, that the enemy had already reached there, had halted, and were busy in killing the cattle belonging to the inhabitants. This rendered it necessary to attack the enemy as soon as possible. On account of the small number of his troops,

Colonel Willett thought it advisable to divide his force; and while one division made a spirited attack in front, the other, performing a circuit through the woods, should attack them in the rear, and thus render the chance of success more probable, than to attack with an inferior force, the enemy's front.

Having come within view of the enemy, the right wing, under Colonel Willett's immediate command, pushed into a field adjoining the one possessed by the enemy, where, opening to the right, and advancing in a line towards them, he pressed them so closely, as caused them to retire to a neighbouring wood. The advance under Colonel Willett immediately began to skirmish, while the remainder of the wing was advancing briskly in two columns. At this time, while the action wore so promising an aspect, without any previous notice, or apparent cause, the whole of this wing turned about and fled, nor was it in his power to rally them. A field-piece, which was left upon a height, at a small distance from the wood, to secure a retreat, was abandoned, and fell into the hands of the enemy. At this critical period, defeat would certainly have ensued, had it not been for the timely succour afforded by Major Rowley, of the state of Massachusetts. Advancing with the left wing, composed wholly of militia, except about sixty levies from his own state, he attacked the enemy with great intrepidity and vigour, in the rear. As it was, the contest was closely disputed until after dark, when the enemy were entirely driven from the field. They retired six miles back into the woods, leaving a great number of their packs behind them, and encamped on the top of a mountain. As for the troops under Colonel Willett, having procured lights, they collected the enemy's wounded, as well as their own, and took about fifty prisoners. In this action, Colonel Willett lost about forty men.

Uncertain as to the route the enemy had taken, two or three days elapsed without any movement of importance. In the mean time, measures were taken to learn the course they intended to take. All, however, that could be discovered, was, that they were penetrating further into the wilderness. From this, Colonel Willett became certain, that they were unable to make any sudden stroke below the Little Falls, and, consequently, on the 27th, took a position on the German Flatts, for the purpose of being between the enemy and their boats, which they had left at Oneida Creek. Here he was joined by sixty warriors of the Oneida tribe, together with some levies and militia, so that his force was augmented to upwards of five hundred men. The 28th was passed in furnishing the choicest of the troops, together with the Indians, with provisions for five days. Toward the close of the same day, it having appeared clearly that the enemy had relinquished all expectation of returning to the boats, and were proceeding either towards Bucks Island or to Oswego, Colonel Willett, taking with him about four hundred troops, besides Indians, commenced anew the pursuit of the enemy. Crossing the Mohawk at Fort Herkimer, the first night, they encamped. The greatest part of the next day they continued their pursuit, through a snow storm, and encamped again at night in a thick wood. About day-light the next morning, a small scout was sent out, and returned in a few minutes with the information, that the enemy were within a short distance of them. Immediately putting the troops under arms, Colonel Willett set out, and in a short time fell in with a small detachment of forty men, with a few Indians. This detachment, it appears, had been ordered to procure a fresh supply of provisions, and were then to follow the track of the main body. Some of this party were killed, some taken, and the rest dispersed. On coming up with the main body, they made a very feeble resistance, showed signs of terror and confusion, and soon set out on a trot, in Indian file. Late in the afternoon, after crossing Canada Creek, where the water was fordable, the enemy showed some signs of resistance, and formed themselves in a body, under the command of Major Walter Butler. At this spot, Major Butler was slain, having received a shot in his eye, which passed through his head: twenty of his men were also slain. After this last show of resistance, the enemy again fled, and were warmly and closely pursued, until night stopped this fatiguing and laborious pursuit. During the night, however, they continued their disorderly flight; and, by this means, gained greatly the start of their pursuers: but, their prospect was most disheartening; indeed, almost certain destruction seemed to await them. Before them was yet a seven days' march, rivers passable only upon rafts, and a barren wilderness in an inclement season of the year. All these difficulties were to be encountered, and overcome, before they could obtain a supply of provisions. To render their situation more deplorable still, in the rapidity of their flight, they had thrown away their packs and blankets, so that they had no covering to protect them from the cold and inclemency of the season.

The enemy having, as has been stated, gained a night's march, and Colonel Willett's troops having provisions only for five days, the Indians and many of the troops having besides in the eagerness of pursuit thrown aside their blankets and provisions, which were now twenty miles in the rear, it was thought unadvisable to fatigue them any longer. The pursuit was therefore relinquished. Col. Willett was farther induced to take this course from the consideration that the enemy were left in a situation in the wilderness, which could hardly have been aggravated by utter defeat or captivity. Besides, had the pursuit continued a day or two longer, the situation of his own troops would have been little better than the enemy's. As it was, the victory was complete, and they were as likely to reap nearly as great benefits from it as if they had succeeded in destroying the enemy.

In this close pursuit, strange as it may appear, notwithstanding the enemy had been four days in the wilderness, with only half a pound of horse flesh per man a day, yet in their famished situation they ran upon a trot, thirty miles before they stopped. The Indians, whom Col. Willett used to consider as the best cavalry for the wilderness, were particularly useful in this pursuit.

The whole of the enemy's loss on this occasion cannot be told. "The fields of Johnstown," says Colonel Willett's official account, "the brooks and rivers, the hills and mountains, the deep and gloomy marshes, through which the enemy had to pass; these must tell—these only can tell their loss." The death of Major Butler, however, in this action, is an occurrence that ought to be particularly noticed. He was a severe scourge on the frontiers. Walter Butler was the son of a Col. Butler, who was Indian agent under Sir William Johnson. This Col. Butler lived on a very fine farm near Johnstown, not far from the Mohawk river, known by the name of Butlersburgh. On this farm Walter was born. He studied law in the city of Albany. Soon after the commencement of the revolutionary war, Sir John, the son of Sir William Johnson, together with Col. Butler, the Indian agent, and their families, and the principal part of the warriors of the Mohawk Indians, went to Canada, and joined the Indians there, who had placed themselves under the protection of the British government. In Canada, Walter procured a lieutenant's commission, in a regular

British regiment. He was with Col. St. Leger, at the siege of Fort Stanwix, in August 1777. After the disastrous battle of General Herkimer, when the great part of the well-affected inhabitants of Tryon county was destroyed, this Walter Butler, with several of the Mohawk Indians, went down into that part of the country, to induce as many of the timid and disaffected of the inhabitants as he could, by large promises and violent threatenings, to join the army under General St. Leger. He was, as we have seen, taken prisoner, tried, and condemned to be hung; but afterwards reprieved, sent to Albany, and confined in the city prison. The winter following, General La Fayette having been appointed to the command of the northern department, some of the inhabitants of the city of Albany, who were acquainted with the family of Butler, and felt a degree of sympathy for Butler himself, petitioned the general to remove him to a more comfortable place of confinement, assuring him that such was the state of his health, he would die if this were not done. Upon this petition, the general consented to take him out of prison, and place him under a guard in a private house; from which he soon made his escape.

The winter following he came from Niagara, with a party of Indians and soldiers, and destroyed the settlement of Cherry Valley. In this expedition Butler was the commander. During the four years that elapsed from Butler's conviction as a spy, to the time of his death, he had exhibited more instances of enterprise, had done more injury, and committed more murders, than any other man on the frontiers. Such was the terror in which he was held by the inhabitants of the frontiers, so cruel a scourge had he been to them, that though Cornwallis's surrender took place about this time, yet the inhabitants expressed more joy at the death of Butler, than the capture of Cornwallis. By a curious coincidence, Col. Willett was judge advocate of the court, at the time Butler was sentenced to be hung as a spy, and now again commander of the party by which he was slain. At his death, he had the same commission in his pocket, which he exhibited at his trial by the court martial.*

So severely was this victory over Major Ross felt, that not only through the rest of the winter, but during the whole of the campaign of 1782, no considerable force of the enemy, in one body, at any time appeared. Bodies of Indians, by scattering, and appearing in small parties, caused considerable trouble, but their attempts were never sufficiently formidable to cause any serious alarm. Frequent accounts, indeed, were brought by individuals, who had discovered straggling parties of Indians, on the most exposed part of the frontiers, which rendered it necessary to use alertness and vigilance ; and frequently to dispatch considerable bodies of troops in the night, several miles into the wilderness, with the hope of falling in with the rear of some of these scattering parties of Indians. These expeditions, though fatiguing and troublesome, and constantly persisted in, effected but little. The timidity or caution of the enemy prevented every exertion that was used to overtake or destroy them; so that the campaign of '82 closed without any important event.

---

* It may be well to note in this place, in relation to the death of Butler, that the account which is given of it in Marshall's Life of Washington, (Appendix to Vol. iv, Note 7,) might lead the reader to infer that there was a degree of cruelty used, contrary to the usages of humane warfare. Mr. Marshall says, "In the party at Canada Creek, was Major Walter Butler, the person who perpetrated the massacre at Cherry Valley. His entreaties for quarter were disregarded, and he fell the victim of that vengeance which his own savage temper had directed against himself :"—whereas it appears, from Col. Willett's narrative, that Butler was shot dead at once; and that there was no time to implore the mercy of the victors.

# CHAPTER VIII.

———•❊ ❊•———

THE inhabitants along the frontiers now began to feel themselves secure. During the year '82, the recruiting of the State troops had been successful, in consequence of the legislatures' having adopted the plan of offering a bounty of money in lieu of the bounty of land : so that at the close of the campaign of '82, Colonel Willett had a regiment of upwards of four hundred State troops.

Winter having set in, barracks for winter quarters were prepared ; and as a considerable number of the troops had not had the small pox, Col. Willett embraced this opportunity of having them inoculated. Having seen the troops sufficiently provided with quarters for the winter, and erected a comfortable log-hut for himself, he set out, toward the last of November, for Albany. He then went to Fishkill for his wife, intending to take her to his quarters with him during the winter. As the head-quarters of General Washington were at Newburgh, directly opposite Fishkill Landing, Col. Willett went to pay his respects to him, and remained to dinner. As soon as dinner was over, he rose to take his leave : the general rose also, and following him out, asked him to go with him into his office. He then inquired as to his success in recruiting, the strength and situation of the regiment : said the clothier-general should have particular orders respecting their clothing; and mentioned that it would be proper to place no reliance on a speedy peace, but be as well prepared as possible for another campaign. He then inquired of Col. Willett if he was acquainted with the situation of the enemy's garrison, at Oswego, and if he thought it might be surprised by an expedition in the winter. This was the first time that an opening ever presented itself to Col. Willett of a chance of procuring fame, that his heart did not vibrate with joy. The expectation he had entertained of spending the winter in comfortable quarters with his family at Fort Rensselaer, was destroyed : but to say any thing that might appear to discourage so important a project, was not in his nature. The conversation finished by the general desiring him to think of the project, and write him his opinion.

Agreeably to General Washington's request, Col. Willett, in about a week after he left him, wrote to him in favour of the enterprise. A correspondence ensued between General Washington and Col. Willett: which correspondence, as it was secret, was in the general's own hand-writing.* All General Washington's orders were strictly observed by Col. Willett; and the utmost precaution used to conceal the design of the expedition.

The troops were suddenly assembled at Fort Herkimer on the 8th day of February. On the 9th, at night, they crossed the Oneida Lake ; and the following day about 2 o'clock, P. M., the troops arrived at Oswego Falls. At this place they went into the woods, and made eight ladders. Their prospects were as promising as they could wish. All the necessary preparations for entering the enemy's works were completed; and every officer was made acquainted

* See these letters of Gen. Washington, in Appendix No. 9.

with the particular part he was to perform. It was scarcely 10 o'clock at night, when the troops reached a point of land about four miles from the fort. Here, on account of the weakness of the ice, they were obliged to take to the land ; and in doing this they had to ascend an eminence, which caused some difficulty in getting up the ladders.

Colonel Willett had procured a young Oneida Indian, called Captain John, and two other Indians, as guides. Not a thought entered his mind of the least danger of losing their way, as they were then but four miles from the fort, and there were still four hours to elapse before the moon set, which was the time fixed upon for entering the fort. Col. Willett's attention was constantly engaged in encouraging the men, whose business it was to carry the ladders ; a labour, which, from the inclemency of the season, the depth of the snow, and the difficulties of the woods, was a very arduous one. His attention being thus occupied, and not having the least apprehension that his guides would lose their way, two hours passed without discovering any opening through the woods, which he had been for some time expecting. This circumstance led him to hasten to the front of the line of march, where he was informed, that the Indian pilot had not been seen for some time, though they were pursuing his track as fast as they could. Colonel Willett immediately set out to follow his track himself, with as quick a step as possible, and in about half an hour overtook him. He found him standing still, and apparently lost and frightened. They had by this time got into a swamp, and some of the men had their feet frozen fast in sunken holes. In this deplorable situation, ignorant where they were, the hope of taking the fort by surprise, vanished ; and the orders of General Washington were peremptory, that if they failed in surprising the fort, the attempt would be unwarrantable. All then that was left for the troops to do, was to retrace their steps. Many of them had suffered much from the frost; only one frozen to death: but a number were lamed, and some so badly, as to require constant assistance to get them along. Such was the gloomy end of an enterprise, which, at ten o'clock at night, presented so fair a prospect of success.

Had they been without a guide, and only taken the precaution to keep in view of the river, they would have had sufficient time between ten o'clock, when they were within four miles of the fort, and the setting of the moon, to have effected the design of the expedition. The failure, therefore, is to be attributed to the guide losing his way. Colonel Willett had been particularly careful to secure the hearty co-operation of the Indian, by assuring him, that he should not be exposed to any danger; that all that was required of him was to conduct them in sight of the fort; and that after it was taken he should have a full share of the plunder. It was not, however, Colonel Willett's opinion, that the Indian led them astray by design, though he put him under guard when he first perceived the situation into which he had led them. It appeared, afterwards, that the mistake of the Indian, originated in his having fallen in with two Indian snowshoe tracks, which he had followed all the day; and as they led in a direct course to Oswego, it was natural to suppose that the travellers were going to that place. The Indian fell in again with these tracks soon after leaving the river, and, following them, was led astray: it was afterwards found, they led to an Indian encampment, some distance down the lake.

During this march to Oswego, congress received advice of the signing the provisional articles of peace; and shortly after Colonel Willett's return to Fort Rensselaer, he went to Albany, where he heard the peace proclaimed by the town-clerk, at the city-hall, to the rejoicing inhabitants.

# CHAPTER IX.

—◦◦◦—

## THE CREEK MISSION.

THE federal constitution having been adopted, and General Washington chosen president, one of his first objects was, forming treaties of peace with the Indians. In the commencement of the president's first term of office, several tribes of Indians were at open war with the United States. Among others, " the Creeks in the south, who could bring into the field six thousand fighting men, were at war with Georgia. In the mind of their leader, the son of a white man, some irritation had been produced by the confiscation of the lands of his father, who had resided in Georgia, and several other refugees from that state, whose property had also been confiscated, contributed still further to exasperate the nation. But the immediate point in contest between them was, a tract of land on the Oconee, which the state of Georgia claimed, under a purchase, the validity of which was denied by the Indians. The regular effective force of the United States was less than six hundred men.*"

To adjust existing differences, and to " negociate a peace with the Creek Indians, General Lincoln, Mr. Griffin, and Colonel Humphreys were sent on a mission into that country. They met M'Gillivray, with several other chiefs,

---

* Marshall, vol. v. p. 181.

and about two thousand men, at Rock Landing on the
Oconee, on the frontiers of Georgia. The treaty commenced with appearances, by no means unfavourable, but
was soon abruptly broken off by M'Gillivray. Some difficulties .arose on the subject of boundary, but the principal
obstacles to a peace were supposed to grow out of his personal interests, and his connections with Spain."*

Upon the failure of this negociation with the Creek Indians,
the Creeks still continuing to manifest a hostile temper, in
some measure, it was supposed, through Spanish influence,
it was thought advisable to make another attempt to avert a
war, " which, should it even extend no further, could be
attended only with public expense, and private calamity."
Still, as an attempt " to renew the pacific overtures which
had already been rejected, unless they could be made under
more favourable circumstances, promised no beneficial result,
and might diminish the respect with which those savages
contemplated the American government, it was resolved,
that the agent to be employed should visit the country on
other pretexts, and should carry a letter of introduction to
M'Gillivray, blending with other subjects, a strong representation of the miseries which a war with the United States
would bring upon his people ; of the indiscretion of breaking
off the negociation at the Rock Landing ; and an earnest
exhortation to repair, with the chiefs of his nation, to the
seat of the federal government, in order to effect a solid and
satisfactory peace. The bearer of this letter was also to be
furnished with passports and letters of safe-conduct, to be
used if the occasion should require them : but he was
instructed not to avow the authority with which he was invested, unless he should be well assured, that the proposition
he was authorised to make would be favourably received."†

---

* Vide Marshall, vol. v. p. 229.    † Vide Marshall, vol. v. p. 273.

In pursuance of this resolution, the day after the arrival of the commissioners from Georgia, with an account of the failure of the negociation, General Knox called upon Colonel Willett, informed him of the circumstance, and the desire of the president to see him, which was complied with. By the president, Colonel Willett was given to understand, that suspicions were entertained that the people of Georgia were not friendly to a peace, but anxious to procure from Congress a force sufficient to subdue them; that by the statement of the secretary of war, it would require fifteen millions of dollars to effect this, and that a considerable portion of the troops were to be furnished from the northern states. The president, at the same time, mentioned it as his opinion, that if a person acquainted with Indians, could enter the country, with such instructions as he would furnish, without the knowledge of the people of Georgia, a war might be prevented, and proper treaties entered into between the United States and the Creek Indians. The president closed with requesting Colonel Willett to undertake the mission.

In conformity with the wish of the president, Colonel Willett engaged in this service. Having, accordingly, received the necessary instructions, and all things being ready, he left New York, March 15th, 1790; embarking on board a sloop, with a servant and two horses, for Charlestown, South Carolina. After a tedious passage of fourteen days, he landed at Charlestown, where lodgings were provided for him by his friend Mr. Adam Gilchrist, in Court Lane. He remained in Charlestown until the 2nd of April, preparing for his journey; on which day he left Chalestown, having the principal part of his baggage in a sulky, in which his servant rode, while he himself went on horseback. The servant whom he carried with him, soon showing signs of fear, he was obliged to send him back to New York, and to fill his place with a German, of whose integrity he was very suspicious.

Having, on the 13th of April, reached General Picken's, whose plantation was situated on the Seneca, a large fork of the Savannah river, he spent a couple of days at his house very agreeably, while the General procured him an Indian, as a guide into the country of the Cherokees. The name of the Indian was Young Corn : he bore a good name ; and his open, manly countenance, corresponded with his character. Here, also, Colonel Willett purchased two additional horses : one for a bow-horse, the other for the Indian to ride.

On Monday, April 19th, at 10 o'clock, A. M., says Colonel Willett, I crossed the Seneca at General Picken's ferry, and commenced the prosecution of my journey into the country of the Indians, accompanied by the Young Corn, and my man John, in the following order :—my guide, the Young Corn, in front, myself next, then the bow-horse, loaded with my baggage, and John in the rear. General Pickens crossed the ferry with me, and then took his leave. From this gentleman and his lady I have received the greatest kindness and civility, and every necessary assistance for the continuance of my journey. I proceeded to Colonel Cloveland's, on the bank of the Tugeloo, where I met with a good harbour for the night.

Tuesday, the 20th, after breakfasting, and crossing the Tugeloo, which is another fork of the Savannah, proceeded according to my yesterday's line of march. Met with a disaster on the road. The bow-horse took fright, ran away, overset his load, and wounded his leg, so that we got only twenty-four miles on our journey. Encamped in the woods, at a branch of good water ; got myself a neat hut built ; supped on chocolate ; and had a very comfortable lodging on my bear-skin and blanket.

13

21st. Took breakfast in camp; mounted at sun-rise, and arrived at Santee at eleven o'clock, A. M. Crossed the mountains to this place in a storm of hail. This is the first of the Cherokee towns on this route; it contains sixteen or eighteen houses, and is surrounded with mountains. The lands are of inferior quality. At this place I purchased corn from the Indians for my horses, and paid in ribands. Continuing my route, passed through a small settlement three miles further on, called Little Chotee, to a small running brook, where I encamped. My day's journey was about twenty-eight miles. Great part of the way much broken and mountainous. Course from Tugeloo to Santee about W. by N., from thence to where I encamped, nearly S. W. A good supper of chocolate, and pleasant night's repose.

On the 22nd, breakfasted and set out by seven o'clock, A. M. Arrived at a town called Huntoweekee, at one o'clock, P. M. This is a new settlement: the town has not been built more than one year. It is situated on both sides a branch of the Cousa river; contains about fifty houses. Here I purchased corn for ribands and paint. Dined in the town; proceeded about eight miles further, crossed the river, and encamped on its bank. Had young corn cut for my horses' fodder. Travelled this day thirty-two miles. While my supper was preparing, was so provoked by my man John, that I had almost put him into the fire. The Indian stared; John was humbled; I drank my chocolate, and went to bed.

23rd. Breakfasted and went on to Long Swamp, or Neueconoheta. This town lies along the bank of a river, called Hitower, which empties into the Cousa. The lands from a few miles above Huntoweekee to this place are very good; and the country appears open. At this place I met Mr. Thomas Gogg, who lives twenty-five miles further on my route, at a town called Pine Log, where he is settled as a trader. I had a letter of introduction from General Pickens to Mr. Gogg, who, in consequence of that letter, returned with me to his town, where I was kindly received by the head man, called Yellow Bird, and several other principal men and women. Travelled this day thirty-five miles. Course, from Little Chotee to Long Swamp, about w. s. w. w., and from thence to Pine Log, w.

24th. After seeing an Indian ball play, went to Euestenaree, where I arrived at three o'clock, P. M. This is the beloved town of the Cherokees, or, in other words, the town of peace, where all transactions relative to peace are discussed and settled. It is likewise a city of refuge. The guilty who fly here, are safe from punishment while they remain in it. No blood may be spilled in this place. It lies along Cousa river, nearly N. W. from Pine Log. The path I travelled to it from that place, runs through a very broken country. I had an introductory letter to the Badger and Jobberson, two Indian chiefs, who reside in this place, by whom I was kindly received. A Mr. Cary, who had long been an interpreter to these people, dwells at this settlement. At his house I found tolerable good quarters, and met with a hospitable reception. I have engaged Mr. Cary and the Jobberson to accompany me to the Creek nation. Here I also learnt, that the shortest and best way for me to go to the Creek nation is to return to the Pine Log, so that I have come thus far out of my way.

April 25th. Lay by at Euestenaree. The day warm, but fair.

26th. Having increased my company, with Mr. Cary and the Jobberson, set out after an early breakfast for the Pine Log. At that place baited my horse and dined. (All these expenses are paid in ribands and paint.) Here took my leave of Mr. Gogg, after paying him six dollars for his services, and proceeded to Hihotee, the last of the Cherokee towns in this quarter. Here I met with a very friendly reception from a Mr. Hughes, a Cherokee half-breed, who is comfortably situated in this town. Travelled this day thirty-five miles. In the afternoon passed over a delightful piece of land. A very fine day.

27th. After breakfasting with Mr. Hughes, crossed the river Hitower in a canoe, and swam the horses. I commenced a new line of march. Mr. Cary in front, next the Jobberson, then myself, then my bow horse, and the Young Corn and John. Travelled twenty-five miles : took a wrong track : had no small difficulty in crossing the woods, through a tract of broken land, to find the right path : lost about five miles. The day and evening pleasant. I was exceedingly distressed with a pain in my stomach. Most of the land bad; considerably stony and hilly.

28th. Had my breakfast, and was mounted by six o'clock in the morning. Crossed this day the Pumkin Posk mountains, which lie about twenty-five miles from Hitower. They are about three miles across, considerably steep, and part of the way difficult to pass. Made a halt from twelve to two o'clock, then went on until near sun-set. Travelled this day thirty-five miles; and encamped at a small running brook. The land passed over in the forenoon, bad ; that in the afternoon, good. Crossed one sharp hill in the afternoon. The rest of the way easy, though something hilly. The day pleasant.

29th. Frost last night. It was some time before the horses were found, but, by steady travelling, made out thirty-five miles. The lands in general good : hills and dales. Most of the hills appear good for wheat ; a few very stony, and a few barren. The timber, chesnut, oak, hickory, ash, poplar, with some maple and beach ; very little under-brush : the path in general easy. Passed two handsome brooks, one about twenty, and the other ten yards wide, within a quarter of a mile of each other. All these waters must enter the Cousa river : they have hard bottoms, and are easy to ford. I observed a large ridge of mountains to the southward.

Friday, April 30th. Proceeded to the first Creek settlement, about twelve miles from which I encamped. From thence I went to a Mr. Scott's, three miles further on, where I met with a hospitable reception. Mr. Scott is a European; has been a trader in this nation for many years, and has considerable property. Here I learnt that Colonel M'Gillivray was at the Oak Fusky, an Indian town, about thirty miles distant, and that he was expected at a Mr. Grierson's, who is likewise a trader, living at the Killebees, eight miles from Mr. Scott's. Mr. Scott accompanied me to Mr. Grierson's, and at six o'clock, p. m. I had the satisfaction of seeing Colonel M'Gillivray arrive at that place. After delivering him my introductory letter, I had some conversation with him; and after a good supper, and most kind entertainment, I went to bed, happy in being under the same roof with the man I have travelled thus far to see. Colonel M'Gillivray appears to be a man of an open, candid, generous mind, with a good judgment, and very tenacious memory. The land I passed over this morning, little better than barren; within the settlement of the Killebees it is good : the day was pleasant. The course from Hitower to the Killebees, about s. w.

The 1st and 2nd of May I remained at Mr. Grierson's : both days pleasant. Here I attended *black drink* for the first time. This is an ancient custom, peculiar to this nation. It is a strong decoction of a leaf, called Kasina. The leaf is parched before it is boiled. This custom carries with it an appearance of a religious nature. It is very ceremonious. The drink is usually boiled in the centre of a square, set apart in every town, near what is commonly called the Hot-house. The square consists of four rows of seats, from forty to fifty yards long, fronting each other, leaving an opening at each angle for entrance. The seats are neatly matted with reed, and covered with bark. They are ten or twelve feet deep, rising higher in the rear than in the front, so as to give each person as he sits, an opportunity of seeing what is doing in the square. The hot-houses are nearly of a circular form, seated in the same manner, and covered close with bark, having only one small door of entrance. The hot-houses are sufficiently large to contain several hundred persons. In these squares and hot-houses all public business is transacted.

When the *black drink* is sufficiently boiled, and ready for use, a principal warrior goes to it, and calls as many men (all of whom must be warriors of eminence) as he may think sufficient to serve the company present with drink. To each of these, the chief warrior hands a gourd filled with the liquor. These men having received the drink, arrange themselves directly in front of the persons intended first to be served; and at a given signal, all together put the gourds filled with the liquor, into the hands of the persons they are respectively to serve, who immediately place it to their mouths, and hold it there, until the servers have sung out two long notes. The gourds are then returned to the servers, who go on to serve the whole company in the same manner, with no other ceremony, except saying to each person, Drink, until the pot of liquor is emptied. But at the commencement of every fresh boiling, the notes are repeated.

During the ceremony of the *black drink*, the chiefs usually exhort the young men to be careful in performing their duties, and admonish them on such subjects as they conceive most beneficial.

In these squares and hot-houses, all their busks are likewise held. Their grand busk is when they receive the
first fruits of their green corn. On this occasion they under-
go purgations and fastings, for four successive days and
nights. At the expiration of this term all the fires in the
town are put out, and a new fire made by the friction of two
pieces of wood. This new fire is carried to every house in
the village. On this solemn occasion all former offences
are forgiven. The purgations and fastings are considered
as expiatory; and with the new fire a new friendship com-
mences among all persons.

Monday, 3d of May, set out from Mr. Grierson's, accompanied by Col. M'Gillivray, his servant, and all the company
I brought with me from the country of the Cherokees, except Young Corn, who lagged behind the day on which I
arrrived at the Killibees, and I have heard nothing from him
since. Mr. Grierson merits my particular acknowledgments
for the attentions and civilities I received from him during
my stay at his house. We went only twelve miles from Mr.
Grierson's to a town called the Fish Pond. In the evening I
attended black drink, and an Indian dance at this town.

On the 4th went to the Hickory Ground, where Colonel
M'Gillivray lives: distance 30 miles. The course from the
Killebees to this place, s. w. The weather was fine: the
land tolerably good.

5th and 6th. Remained at Col. M'Gillivray's: pleasant
weather. The people in the next town are busking for
mulberries.

May 7th. This day Colonel M'Gillivray sent out ten
*broken days* for the chiefs of the lower towns to meet at
Ositchy, in order to consult on my business. (*Broken days*
are a number of sticks sent to the towns intended to be assembled. One of the sticks is thrown away each day, and

when they are all gone, they know it is the time to meet.) This is a pleasant day. In the course of the day, I went to a place called the Apple Grove, five miles from where Col. M'Gillivray lives. This place is improved by M'Gillivray. It is the place of his birth, and is situated, as well as the place where he dwells, on the banks of the Cousa, a very fine river. The Apple Grove is the pleasantest place of the two. At this place I had a delicious regale of strawberries and mulberries. Under the bank by the shore I found a pleasing and delightful recess, where I spent three hours alone. After which I went up to the house, had a dinner of fish, and returned home.

8th. Took a walk to see the old French Alabama fort: or rather the place where it stood, on the banks of the Cousa: for there is scarcely a trace of it to be seen at present. About two miles lower down is the conflux of this, and the Toloposa rivers: at which place they form the river Mobile, which empties itself into the Gulf of Florida, about 60 miles west of Pensacola.

Sunday the 9th. There was a light rain. This is the first rain I have seen since the 21st of last month. I remained here all day.

10th, was a rainy day; notwithstanding which, I went to see a ball play.

On the 11th there were several heavy showers. I was very busy preparing for my journey to the treaty.

Wednesday, May 12th. At 9 o'clock A. M., set out for the lower towns in company with M'Gillivray, his servant and my own, to attend the treaty. Reached Mr. Carnell's, the interpreter, who lives at Tuckabatchy, at 4 o'clock, P. M., a distance of 25 miles. On our way we had a shower of rain. Course the first half day south east; the other half about east. The greater part of the lands we passed over were good; some very good.

13th. We crossed the Toloposa, accompanied by the interpreter, and proceeded to the Talline Kings: distance 20 miles. On our way stopped at Mr. M'Queen's, an old Scotchman, who said he had been a trader in this nation between fifty and sixty years. The day following set out for the Hallowing Kings, where we arrived at 2 o'clock, P. M. The course of these two days about E. S. E. : a light sandy soil : country open and level.

15th. Thunder and rain last night; went to the Cowetas; road good, land bad; weather warm. Put up at Mr. Deresau's, who is a trader at this place. It is a numerous settlement. A rum drinking among the Indians: of course troublesome.

Sunday 16th. Heavy thunder and rain great part of the night. At two o'clock, P. M., for the town of Ositchy; arrived there at 6 : warm weather : the road and land in general good. This town, as well as the Cowetas and Eueschetas and many others, lie along the banks of the Chotohotchy river, which runs into the Gulph of Florida.

Monday 17th. Attended *black drink* at the square in this town, with the chiefs, who were assembled agreeably to the order of the broken days, at 11 o'clock A. M. Delivered them the following speech.

Brothers:—I am come to you from our beloved town by order of our beloved chief, George Washington, to invite you to a treaty of peace and friendship at a council fire in our beloved city.

Brothers: Our beloved chief, who wishes prosperity to the red people, as well as to the white, has directed me to advise you that he is very desirous of forming a lasting treaty of peace and amity with your nation. That in

14

order to do this effectually, it is his wish to have his own name, and the name of your beloved chief, fixed to the treaty, that it may be strong and lasting.

Brothers : I am very pointedly instructed to inform you that the United States want none of your lands : that effectual measures will be taken to secure them all to you by our beloved chief; who has an arm sufficiently strong to punish all such as may presume to act contrary to any treaty which he, in conjunction with your beloved chief, may make

Brothers : Our beloved chief is ready to agree with your beloved chief to secure to you your lands : to promote your trade by affording you means of procuring goods in a cheap and easy way; and to do all such things as will contribute to promote the welfare and happiness of your nation.

Brothers : I stand before you, a messenger of peace. It is your interest, and it is our interest, that we should live in peace with each other. I promise myself, that you will attend to this friendly invitation ; and that your beloved chief, with such other of your chiefs and warriors as you may choose for that purpose, will repair with me to the council fire, that is kindled in our beloved town, that we may form a treaty, which shall be strong as the hills, and lasting as the rivers.

After withdrawing for one hour, I was called in, and received the following answer.

Brother : We are glad to see you. You have come a great way ; and as soon as we fixed our eyes upon you, we were made glad. We are poor, and have not the knowledge of white people.

Brother : Our fathers have told us, whenever any white people came among us, we should take them by the hand, and use them well. We have always followed their advice.

Brother: We were invited to a treaty at the Rock Landing: we went there—nothing was done: we were disappointed, and came back with sorrow.

Brother: You say, you come from your beloved chief,
George Washington, to invite our beloved chief to a council
fire, in your beloved town. The road is very long, and the
weather is very hot; but our beloved chief will go with you,
and such other chiefs and warriors as shall be appointed for
that purpose will go with him.

Brother: All that our beloved chief shall do, we will
agree to. We wish you may be preserved from every evil.
We will count the time our beloved chief is away; and
when he comes back, we shall be very glad to see him,
with a treaty, that shall be as strong as the hills, and last
as long as the rivers.

The business at this place being finished to our mutual
satisfaction, returned into Deresau's, where we arrived at
six o'clock. Had a heavy shower of rain by the way.

The day following remained at Mr. Deresau's. The afternoon was rainy.

19th. Left Deresau's, after a late breakfast; travelled
until near sun-set, and encamped in the woods. Had
several showers of rain by the way.

20th. Started very early; halted and breakfasted at the
Tame Kings: then proceeded to Mr. Carrel's, at Tucka-
batchy. This is a fine settlement. The lands are very
good; the prospect along the banks of the river has a pleasing effect, and all nature seems to conspire to make this a
most agreeable settlement.

21st. This morning I took black drink with the chiefs,
who had assembled from the upper town, and delivered
my talk to them; after which, I received the following
answer.

Brother: You tell us you come from your beloved chief, George Washington, to invite us to a council fire, in your beloved town; to make a peace, that shall last as long as the rivers.

Brother: We are willing to be at peace. We love to stay at home, and mind our hunting. We were invited to a treaty at the Rock Landing; we went there; we were made fools of, and came back without doing any thing.

Brother: We did not mean to go to any more treaties with your people; but you have come a great way, and you speak very good: our beloved chief, and such other chiefs and warriors as may be chosen, will go with you; and we will agree to all they may do.

At Ositchy, the answer was delivered by the Hallowing King, who is a fine looking man, and a great orator; and at Tuckabatchy, it was delivered by a half-breed, called the White Lieutenant, a very respectable chief, a venerable looking man, and a good speaker.

Having finished our business in the square at Tucka-batchy, with the same success as at Ositchy, we returned to Mr. Carnel's; took breakfast, and set out for Colonel M'Gillivray's, at which place we arrived at six o'clock, P. M., having had a shower of rain by the way.

Saturday, May 22nd. This day I wrote to the secretary of war, and sent my letter by Mr. Cary, for which, and his other services, I paid forty dollars. The Jobberson returned home, before I went to the lower town. The day very pleasant.

Saturday, May 29th. This day I crossed the Toloposa, and went five miles to see a most superb ball play. There were about eighty players on a side. The men, women, and children, from the neighbouring towns, were assembled upon this occasion. Their appearance was splendid: all the paths leading to the place were filled with people; some on foot, some on horseback. The play was conducted with as much order and decorum as the nature of things would admit of. The play is set on foot by one town sending a challenge to another; if the challenge be accepted, the time and place are fixed on, and the whole night before the play is employed by the parties in dancing, and some other ceremonious preparations. On the morning of the play, the players on both sides paint and decorate themselves, in the same manner as when they are going to war. Thus decorated, and stripped of all such clothing as would encumber them, they set out for the appointed field. The time of their arrival is so contrived, that the parties arrive near the field at the same time; and when they get within about half a mile, in a direction opposite to each other, you hear the sound of the war song and the yell; when, presently, the parties appear in full trot, as if fiercely about to encounter in fight. In this manner they meet, and soon become intermingled together, dancing while the noise continues. Silence then succeeds: each player places himself opposite to his antagonist. The rackets which they use are then laid against each other, in the centre of the ground appointed for the game. They then proceed to measure a distance of three hundred yards, one hundred and fifty each way, from the centre, where they erect two poles, through which the ball must pass, to count *one*. The play is commenced by the balls being thrown up in the air, from the centre; every player, then, with their rackets, of which each has two, endeavours to catch the ball, and throw it between the poles; each side labouring to throw it between the poles towards their own towns; and every time this can be accomplished, it counts one. The game is usually from twelve to twenty. This was lost by the challengers. Large bets are made upon these occasions; and great strength, agility, and dexterity are displayed. The whole of the present exhibition was grand, and well conducted. It sometimes happens, that the inhabitants of a town game away at these plays all their clothes, ornaments, and horses. Throughout the whole of the game, the women are constantly on the alert, with bottles and gourds filled with drink, watching every opportunity to supply the players. The day was fair; and I returned home, much pleased with the amusement.

On Tuesday, the 1st of June, at eleven o'clock in the morning, I set out from Colonel M'Gillivray's house, at Little Tallasee, on my return for New York, accompanied by Colonel M'Gillivray, his nephew and two servants, with eight warriors belonging to the Upper Creeks, my man John, and several bow, and some spare horses.

June 9, at nine o'clock, A. M., arrived at the Stony Mountains, about eight miles from which we encamped. Here we found the Cowetas and Curatas, to the number of eleven, waiting for us. Lay by until three o'clock, P. M., then proceeded eight miles, and encamped by a large creek of the waters of the Oak Mulgee. Course in general nearly E. N. E. Pleasant day: shower of rain after we encamped. While I was at the Stony Mountains I ascended the summit. It is one solid rock, of a circular form, about a mile across. Many strange tales are told by the Indians of this mountain. I have now passed all the Indian settlements, and shall only observe, that the inhabitants of these countries appear very happy; and while the red and white alternately blend in their countenances, health and fragrance breathe around.

June 14th. We arrived at Hopewell; crossed the Seneca river at General Picken's Ferry: distance twenty miles: pleasant day. Here we received a most hearty welcome.

15th. Fair weather. At Hopewell the Tallisee king arrived, with other Indians, from the middle towns: the ———— overtook us by the way, with one more from the upper towns. The great Notchy warrior also arrived, with three more from the Notches.

Friday, June 18th. Left General Picken's at ten o'clock. Twenty-six of the Indians, in three waggons, and four on horseback; Colonel M'Gillivray, his nephew, two servants, and the interpreter, with my man, were likewise on horseback, and myself in my sulky. General Picken accompanied us as far as Mr. Hambleton's, fifteen miles, where we put up for the night.

Sunday, June 27th, we proceeded to Guilford Court-house, and took quarters at Captain Dent's. About two hours after we arrived at this place, Colonel M'Gillivray was visited by a Mrs. Brown, who had formerly been a prisoner in the Creek nation. She was captured, with several of her children, by a party of Indians, who at the same time killed her husband. She was redeemed from her captivity by Colonel M'Gillivray, with whom she afterwards lived twelve months. The meeting was truly affecting.

At nine o'clock, on the morning of July the 6th, I arrived at Richmond, where I had a dinner provided for the Indians, who came in at three o'clock in the afternoon. At this place I remained the 7th, 8th, and 9th. During our stay at Richmond we were treated with the greatest attention. On the 8th, Colonel M'Gillivray and myself dined in the academy with the governor, council, judges, a number of the gentlemen of the bar, and other persons of distinction.

9th. On our arrival at Fredericksburgh, we were hurried to the theatre, and, notwithstanding the entire derangement of our plan, for the prosecution of our journey, we could not avoid remaining at that place all day. Dined at a public dinner with the chiefs. Visited Mrs. Lewis, the sister of our president, and several others of his relations. Viewed the place in which he was bred, and the cottage in which his mother died.

Saturday 17th. Set out for Philadelphia; was met by a message from the president and council of Pennsylvania, expressing a desire that I should halt at Gray's Ferry. After halting and refreshing, for two or three hours, we were escorted into the city. In the evening, returned to Gray's gardens, to see the exhibition there.

Monday, 19th July. This day was taken up in paying visits. The Indians were shewn a great many curiosities in and about Philadelphia; visited, formally, by a committee from the society of Friends. Had a public dinner: was at the theatre at night.

On Tuesday, the 20th, left Philadelphia, at the dawn of day; arrived at Elizabeth-town Point at four o'clock in the afternoon, from which place, just at dusk, I set out for New York, in a row-boat. Landed at White-hall dock, between nine and ten o'clock. Set out again for Elizabeth-town Point, at two o'clock in the morning, at which place I arrived at six o'clock, where I found a sloop, which had been sent from New York, ready to transport us to that place. Embarking on board of the sloop, with the Indians, for New York, we landed about noon, near the Coffee-house, and were received, with great splendour, by the Tammany society, in the dress of their order; conducted up Wall-street, passed the Federal Hall, where congress were in session, and with much pomp and parade, escorted to the president's. After their introduction to the president, the Indians, with additional parade, visited the minister of war, and governor Clinton;

and then repaired to the City Tavern, where an elegant entertainment finished the day.*

---

\* On the first information, at St. Augustine, that M'Gillivray was about to
repair to New York, the intelligence was communicated to the governor at
Havanna, and the secretary of East Florida came to New York, with a large
sum of money, to purchase flour, as it was said, but to embarrass the negotiations with the Creeks, was believed to be his real design.

He was closely watched, and measures were taken to render any attempts
he might make, abortive.—*See Marshall's Life of Washington*, vol. **v.** p. **274.**

# CHAPTER X.

—◦◦◦◦—

## CONCLUSION.

IMMEDIATELY after the war, in the year '84, Col. Willett was appointed Sheriff of the city and country of New York: which office he held for a term of four years. After his return from the Creek Mission, he was again, in the year '92, appointed to the same office; and held it for another term of four years. In this year, also, he was appointed brigadier-general in the army which was intended to operate against the hostile tribes, north west of the Ohio. The following letters from Gen. Knox, at that time Secretary of War, refer to this appointment.

WAR DEPARTMENT, *April* 12*th,* 1792.

SIR:—I have the honour to inform you, that the President of the United States, by and with the advice and consent of the Senate, has appointed you a brigadier-general in the army of the United States.

You will please immediately to signify your acceptance or non-acceptance of this appointment:—in case of your acceptance you will repair to Philadelphia, with all possible dispatch.

In order that you may judge of the pay, rations, and emoluments for the commissioned and non-commissioned officers, and privates in the service of the United States, I enclose you the act of Congress relative to the military establishment.

I have the honor to be,

Sir,

Your most obedient servant,

KNOX.

*Secretary of War.*

*Brig.-Gen. Marinus Willett.*

-------

[ *Private.* ]

*Philadelphia, April 12th 1792.*

MY DEAR SIR,—You will herewith receive official information of your appointment of Brigadier-General.

The officers are,

    Anthony Wayne, *Major-General.*

    Daniel Morgan, *Brigadier-General.*

    Marinus Willett,   ditto.   ditto.

    John Brooks,       ditto.   ditto.

    James Wilkinson, is nominated for the fourth brigadier-general, not yet appointed.

It has been said that the acceptance of Morgan is doubtful. Of this I can say nothing. But if he should decline, then you would be second in command.

I have been anxious for your appoint on this occasion, being convinced of your talents to render service to your country and honour to yourself. Let me hear from you by the return of the post.

Yours sincerely,

KNOX.

*Colonel Willett.*

Before Colonel Willett received the above official notification, he wrote the following letter to General Washington, with the intention of stopping the appointment.

*New York,* 14*th April,* 1792.

Sir,—A report has reached me, in a way I cannot doubt of, that I am in nomination for the office of brigadier-general. This is a fresh instance of the estimation in which I stand with you, and of course very flattering to me. The repeated instances of your regard, which I have experienced, are convincing evidences of your desire to promote my welfare. It is therefore with regret I find myself nominated for an office, which, under existing circumstances, would operate to my disadvantage. My desire to serve my country is not abated; yet when I reflect upon my present situation, and the nature of the service which the appointment would require of me, I am led to decline engaging in it; and flatter myself this step will not be disapproved of by you.

It has been my uniform opinion, that the United States ought to avoid an Indian war. I have generally conceived this to be our wisest policy. The reasons alledged in support of the present Indian war, have never brought conviction to my mind. From my knowledge and experience of these people, I am clear that it is not a difficult thing to preserve peace with them. That there are bad men among them, and that these will at times do acts which deserve punishment, is very clear. But I hold, that to go to war, is not the proper way to punish them. Most of the Indians that I have had any knowledge of, are conceited and vain. By feeding their vanity you gain their good opinion; and this in time procures their esteem and affection. By conciliating their good will, you will render them susceptible of almost any impression. They are credulous, yet suspicious.

They think a great deal; and have in general good notions
of right and wrong. They frequently exhibit proofs of
grateful minds; yet they are very revengeful. And though
they are not free from chicanery and intrigue, yet if their
vanity is properly humored, and they are dealt justly by, it
is no difficult matter to come to reasonable terms with them.
The intercourse I have had with these people, the treat-
ment I have myself received from them, and which I
have known others to receive, makes me an advocate for
them. To fight with them, would be the last thing I should
desire. And yet, Sir, I declare, from the experience I have
had, I do not conceive it difficult to beat them, when
brought to action. When in small parties they scatter
themselves along a frontier, they have always been found
exceedingly troublesome and dangerous. This kind of warfare is their forte; and in it, they are found to be truly tre-
mendous. But when they attempt any thing in large bodies,
I have found, notwithstanding their great dexterity in the
wilderness, and the advantage they usually derive from the
admirable position they take, that they are easily beat.
In marching through woods, where troops are exposed to
attacks from Indians, particular attention should be paid
not only to the mode and line of march, but also to extend
small parties and single men far on the flanks in front and
in rear. But whenever a serious attack is made, which is
usually furious, an instantaneous charge, with huzzaing,
sufficiently loud to drown the noise the Indians make, will
never fail to repel them. And this stroke repeated and pursued, will, I am well convinced, terminate in victory. And
yet victory even over Indians is generally paid for: but defeats are terrible. The honour, however, of fighting and beating Indians, is what I do not aspire after. If in any way
I could be instrumental in effecting and maintaining peace

with them, it would be to me a source of great gratification.
I have the honor to be your Excellency's
obedient humble servant.
                                   MARINUS WILLETT.
*To the President of the United States.*

Colonel Willett having declined the appointment of brigadier-general, he was shortly after requested to attend, in a
pacific character, a great council, which was to be held
at the Miami village, in order, if possible, to effect a peace
between the Indians and the United States. The duties of
his office, however, which at that time were very arduous
and important, led him to decline this offer. The following
is General Knox's letter on this subject.

[*Private and confidential.*]
*War Department,* 18*th April,* 1792.

SIR,—It was with regret I read your letter of ——————,
declining the acceptance of the commission of a brigadier-
general : but you have the right to be perfectly master of
your own conduct.

The president of the United States has showed me your
letter of the 14th instant, wherein you express your ideas of
an Indian war. Be assured, that nothing can be more
disagreeable to him and the government. But the present
hostilities originated in the war with Great Britain, and that
they continued without intermission, and increased from
time to time, until they became too enormous to be longer
overlooked by government, cannot be doubted by any impar-
tial man, who will attend to the evidence.

But, notwithstanding the past, it is the desire of the
president of the United States, to terminate it without the
further effusion of blood : preparatory overtures have been

made to the Indians, who are to have a great council at the Miami village the next month.

But a person of character, intelligence, and address, is required to be present at that council, in behalf of the United States, to unfold in terms which the Indians will comprehend,

First, that we require no lands but those which we conceive to have been fairly purchased, of those tribes who had a right to sell.

Secondly, that if any of the tribes can show just right to any lands they claim, by virtue of the said treaties, they shall be liberally compensated for such right.

Thirdly, that we are not only willing to be at peace with all nations, but to impart to them such of the blessings of civilization as will suit their condition.

Fourthly, it is conceived, were they convinced of the truth of those sentiments, that peace must be the consequence. But, the difficulty is, to find a suitable character. You have been applied to, and declined. It would appear, however, from your letter to the president, that you would seem still to be desirous of being of service to your country, at this time.

I am authorized to assure you, that if you will still undertake the business, in which, from the preparatory measures, I can assure you there will be but little personal hazard, (although that would not be a consideration with you,) that you would render your country a most acceptable service. That if you succeed, of which I should flatter myself, you will have the glory thereof, besides being most liberally compensated, in a pecuniary way, which shall be stipulated to your satisfaction.

If you should incline to undertake this affair, not a moment of time should be lost in repairing here. The way would be by Pittsburg, down to Fort Washington; every facility of guards would be afforded you. Captain Hendricks, and perhaps others of the Indians, here present, might accompany you. Besides, there are women prisoners at Fort Washington, and, probably, friendly Wabash Indians, who would accompany you.

Permit me to urge your compliance with this invitation to perform the mission, and that you would, immediately and explicitly, inform me of your determination.

I am, Sir, with great respect,

Your most obedient humble servant,

KNOX.

*Colonel Marinus Willett.*

To this letter, Colonel Willett made the following reply.

*New York, April 21st, 1792.*

SIR,—I have been honoured with your letter of the 18th instant. I do indeed feel myself disposed, as I trust I always shall be, to render to my country every service in my power; nor is it possible for me to express the satisfaction I should receive in seeing an end of the present unhappy Indian war. The desire of the president of the United States, to bring about a peace, on terms of equity, and to prevent the further effusion of blood, are so consonant to my mind, that had it not been for the disagreeable and disorderly appearances in this city, arising from the numerous bankruptcies which have lately taken place, I should have been induced to set out immediately for the seat of the general government, with a view of rendering every aid in my power to bring about so desirable an object. But there never was a time when the exercise of the powers of the office, which I now hold, appeared more requisite for the preservation of good order. I cannot, therefore, think of absenting myself, until appearances become more favourable.

Be assured, sir, that I have a high sense of the honour done by the president of the United States, in this mark of his confidence, and, that

I am, with great respect,

Your most obedient servant,

MARINUS WILLETT.

In the year 1807, he was appointed Mayor of the city of New York, which office he held one year.

During the last war, though unable, through the infirmities of age, to take an active part in it, he yet laboured to promote a spirit of patriotism, and military ardour, among his fellow-citizens. His speech at the great meeting in the Park will be found in the Appendix.*

One of the last acts in which Colonel Willett appeared as a public character, was that of chairman of the Greek committee. Extracts from his speech on that occasion will be found in the Appendix.†

During, however, the last years of his life, Colonel Willett mingled but little in public affairs. Surrounded by his family and friends, he yielded slowly, but not reluctantly, to the gradual progress of decay. He had outlived his generation, and found, from his own experience, as he often expressed it, the truth of the Psalmist's declaration : " The days of our years are three-score years and ten ; and if by reason of strength they be four-score years, yet is their strength labour and sorrow ; for it is soon cut off, and we fly away." His mind was constantly fixed upon his approaching change. With the greatest humility, but at the same time with the most lively feelings of piety, did he acknowledge the astonishing mercy of God, in devising a

---

* See Appendix, No. 10.　　　† See Appendix, No. 11.

plan of salvation through an infinite Redeemer, so mercifully adapted to the fallen and miserable condition of the human family. His only hope of salvation rested upon repentance toward God, and faith in our Lord Jesus Christ.

He was seized a few months prior to his decease with an attack of paralysis, from which he entirely recovered. His constitution was, however, much enfeebled; and the occasional use of medicine was required to remove constipation. The absence of his physician induced him to neglect the use of the required remedies, and a diarrhœa followed, which prostrated his strength, and terminated his life, on Sunday, the 23d of August, 1830, in the ninety-first year of his age.

————

Upon the news of Col. Willett's death, the following resolutions were passed in the Common Council, and transmitted to his widow, accompanied with the annexed letter from the Mayor.

*Mayor's Office, City Hall, August 24th,* 1830.

MADAM,—In obedience to the directions of the Common Council of the city of New York, I fulfil the melancholy duty of transmitting to you the enclosed resolutions, which the death of your husband, our much lamented fellow-citizen, Col. Marinus Willett, has called forth.

Permit me, Madam, to unite my own feelings of sympathy and sorrow with those of the Common Council, on the heavy bereavement with which it has pleased an all-wise God to afflict you and your family, and to assure you that his memory will always be cherished by me with the deepest veneration.

I have the honour to be, Madam,

Your most obedient Servant,

WALTER BOWNE, Mayor.

*Mrs. Marinus Willett.*

In Common Council, August 23d, 1830.

His Honor, the Mayor, having announced to the Board the death of Col. Marinus Willett, the Recorder offered the following resolutions, which were adopted *unanimously.*

Resolved, That the Common Council entertain for the memory of Col. Marinus Willett, the most profound respect. That they remember with grateful recollection the eminent public services of the deceased. His patriotism and devotion to his country—his achievements in the war of the revolution—his valor in battle—his heroic firmness in the most dangerous of military enterprises, and his early, constant, and unshaken support to the great cause of American independence.

Nor is the Common Council unmindful of the strong claims which the deceased has upon the respectful feelings of his fellow-citizens, for the able, upright, and enlightened manner in which he discharged his *civil* duties, in the various important public stations which he filled.

Resolved, That as a tribute of respect to the virtues of Col. Marinus Willett, the Corporation of the city of New York will assemble at the Common Council Chamber, in the City Hall, at 4 o'clock to-morrow afternoon, and will from thence proceed to attend the funeral of the deceased.

Resolved, That a copy of the preceding resolutions, with the condolence of the Common Council, be transmitted by his Honor, the Mayor, under the corporate seal, to the family of Col. Willett.          WALTER BOWNE, Mayor.

————

In the Court for the trial of Impeachments and the Correction of Errors, held on Tuesday, August 24th, 1830, the death of Col. Willett being announced, Chief Justice Savage offered the following order, prefaced with some appropriate remarks, which was unanimously adopted.

Ordered, That this court, in testimony of their esteem for the memory of Col. Willett, and of their admiration of his patriotic conduct and distinguished services in the revolution, and of the ability and integrity with which he discharged the duties of the various and important civil offices to which he has been called by the authority of his country, attend his funeral, and that this order be entered on the minutes of this court.

————

Numerous other public testimonials\* of respect were paid to the memory of Col. Willett, which showed the deep feeling produced by his death among the community at large.

The funeral of Col. Willett took place on Tuesday afternoon, the 24th of August. "The coffin was conveyed into the garden in the rear of his dwelling, under an arbour: a gate was thrown open in the rear, so that the great number of visitors who were anxious to view his remains might pass through without confusion. It was computed that not less than ten thousand persons availed themselves of the opportunity.

"The coffin was made of cedar, which Col. Willett had provided for the purpose about ten years before, in which the body was placed, habited, at his request, in his ordinary dress, with his hat on.

"The procession formed at his residence at Cedar Grove, in Broome street. The pall-bearers were Col. Troup, Col. Fish, Col. Trumbull, Col. A. Ogden, Major General Morton, Major Fairlie, J. Pintard, Esq. and Mr. Dominick. The bier was attended by the members of the Cincinnati Society, the members of the Court of Errors, the members of the Common Council, the Judges of the different Courts, together

————

\* See Appendix, No. 18.

with an immense concourse of citizens in carriages and on foot, accompanied by a troop of horse, and a corps of New York state artillery. The procession moved from his residence to Trinity Church; and the remains were deposited in his family vault in Trinity church-yard. During the afternoon, ninety minute-guns were fired on the Battery, and volleys of musketry over the grave."

The following extract of a letter from Dr. Marinus Willett, the eldest son of Col. Willett, to his wife, in relation to the death and funeral of his parent, will give the reader a touching and vivid account of the melancholy but interesting scene.

" We have seen his eyes which so often beamed with affection, and his lips which so often conveyed to us the feelings of a heart beating with ardent attachment, closed for ever; while every thing with us remains as before, except the sad void which his absence has produced. No longer do I see him occupy his well-known chair: no more do I aid his vision when I approach him by the mention of my name: no more do I receive his affectionate greetings: no longer am I called upon to make those particular inquiries about his health, which I have been wont daily to do. No: he is no longer seen among us.

"The last time I saw his face, he was lying in his coffin, clad in his ordinary clothes, and wearing his large black hat. (How often have I seen him reposing his aged and wearied limbs on the sofa, looking very much as he then looked.) He was lying under those trees and vines in the garden, where he has spent so much of his time this summer, enjoying with great gratification the gradual growth of those melons and peaches, of which he was extravagantly fond. How often, as he sat in his chair, in the same place, have I watched him as he enjoyed his tranquil sleep. Here now his aged companions wept over him : here an affectionate and respectful neighbourhood gazed at him with countenances marked with sorrow ; and more than ten thousand of his fellow-citizens, who had assembled to pay the last tribute of respect to his memory, passed in regular procession by his remains. All was still and solemn. Our friend, Dr. De Witt, made a prayer, in which, with the feeling you would expect from a man of his character, who was at the same time the son of one of my father's officers, he alluded with true eloquence to his age, his piety, his services, and the blessing which they conferred upon his country : closing with a devout acknowledgment to God for all the blessings he had conferred upon him.

" After the procession began to move, and when the hearse arrived at the gate, the troops passed before it, and their solemn and delightful music, with plaintive and funereal notes, soothed the soul with its solemn melancholy. Slowly the procession moved along through streets thronged with spectators ; and did not arrive at the Trinity Church until it was quite dark. The coffin was taken from the hearse some distance from the church, and surrounded by his old brother officers. We followed it through a double rank of soldiers into the church. The solemn martial music—the darkness of the night—the appearance of the soldiers—and the sombre aspect of the church and grave-yard, while we followed our dear parent, produced the most overpowering sensations. After the service had been read by Mr. Anthon, we passed slowly and sadly through the burying-ground, guided by the dim light of the torch to the tomb. Never did I expect to see such a true exhibition of the scene described in that incomparable description of the funeral of Sir John Moore. The drum—the dim light of the taper—

the distant minute-gun—his martial cloak around him—with the volleys of musketry, and the cold and silent tomb—all were associated with the circumstance that I was paying the last tribute of respect to so loved and excellent a parent; and produced feelings of sorrow, which a strong confidence that he was then enjoying the bliss of the redeemed, could alone render tolerable."

# APPENDIX.

## No. I.*

"Loudon was superseded in the beginning of 1758, by General Abercrombie; but the colonies cannot be said to have gained much by the substitution. The new commander-in-chief wasted a part of their resources, and checked the momentum of the mighty force which Pitt had arrayed on this continent against the French, by an ill-advised and ill-managed expedition against Crown Point. He took with him *six thousand men,* of whom nine thousand were provincials, and urged them to a hopeless assault upon Ticonderoga, which cost the lives of more than sixteen hundred of his bravest European troops, and of four hundred provincials. 'This attack,' says the Universal History, 'when no prospect of success could possibly present itself, was followed by a retreat as pusillanimous as the other was presumptuous. The General re-embarked the troops, and though an incident had happened that might not have been easily foreseen, or rationally expected, he returned to his former camp at Lake George.' "

## No. II.†

"Anxious to repair in any way the mischief and disgrace of this repulse, Abercrombie consented, at the solicitation of a *native American* officer, Colonel Bradstreet, to detach him with three thousand men, against Fort Frontenac, on the north side of the Ohio. This body of troops, with the ex-

---

ception of only one hundred and fifty-five regulars, was composed of provincials ; and after surmounting, as the historians acknowledge, incredible difficulties and hardships, it gave an earnest of victory to the British cause, by capturing the fortress, together with nine armed vessels, a vast quantity of ammunition, &c., and breaking up thus the principal depot of supplies for the north-western posts, and the hostile Indians."

No. III.

HARTFORD, AUGUST 21ST, 1777.

*The following is a Narrative of part of the Transactions at and near Fort Stanwix, since the investiture of that place by the Enemy, given in Manuscript by Lieutenant-Colonel Willett, of that Garrison.*

On Saturday evening, August 2d, five battoes arrived with stores for the garrison. About the same time we discovered a number of fires a little better than a mile from the north-west corner of the fort. The stores were all got safe in, and the troops which were a guard to the battoes marched up. The captain of the battoes, and a few of his men, delaying their time about the boats, were fired on by a party of Indians, which killed one man and wounded two ; the captain himself was taken a prisoner.

Next morning the enemy appeared in the edge of the woods about a mile below the fort, where they took post in order to invest it upon that quarter, and to cut off the communication with the country ; from whence they sent in a flag who told us of their great power, strength, and determination, in such a manner as gave us reason to suppose they were not possessed of strength sufficient to take the fort : Our answer was a determination to support it.

All day on Monday we were much annoyed by a sharp fire of musketry from the Indians and German rifle-men, which, as our men were obliged to be exposed on the works, killed one and wounded seven. The day after the firing was not so heavy, and our men under better cover; all the damage was one man killed by a rifle ball. This evening indicated something in contemplation by the enemy. The Indians were uncommonly noisy; they made most horrid yellings great part of the evening in the woods hardly a mile from the fort. A few cannon were fired among them.

Wednesday morning there was an unusual silence. We discovered some of the enemy marching along the edge of the woods downwards. About eleven o'clock three men got into the fort, who brought a letter from General Harkaman of the Tryon county militia, advising us that he was at Eriska, (8 miles off,) with part of his militia, and proposed to force his way to the fort for our relief. In order to render him what service we could in his march, it was agreed that I should make a sally from the fort with 250 men, consisting of one half Gansevoorts, one half Massachusetts ditto, and one field piece (an iron three pounder.) The men were instantly paraded, and I ordered the following disposition to be made; thirty men for the advance guard, to be commanded by Capt. Van Benscouton, and Lieutenant Stockwell; thirty for the rear guard under the command of Captain Allen, of Massachusetts troops, and Lieutenant Deuffendorf; thirty for flank guards, to be commanded by Captain ——, from Massachusetts, and Ensign Chase. The main body formed into eight subdivisions commanded by Captain Blacker, Lieutenants Comine, Bogardus, McClenner, Coffraunder; Ensigns Begley, Lewis, and Dennison; Lieutenant Ball, the only supernumerary officer, to march with me. Captain Jansen to bring up the rear of the main body. Captain Swartwoudt, with Ensigns Magee, Ament, and 50 men, to guard the field piece, which was under the direction of Major Bedlow.

Nothing could be more fortunate than this enterprise.

We totally routed two of the enemy's encampments, destroyed all the provisions that were in them, brought off upwards of 50 brass kettles, and more than 100 blankets, (two articles which were much needed,) with a quantity of muskets, tomahawks, spears, ammunition, clothing, deerskins, a variety of Indian affairs, and five colours, (the whole of which on our return to the fort were displayed on our flag staff under the continental flag.) The Indians took chiefly to the woods, the rest of the troops then at their posts to the river. The number of men lost by the enemy is uncertain. Six lay dead in their encampments, two of which were Indians; several scattered about in the woods; but their greatest loss appeared to be in crossing the river, and an inconsiderable number upon the opposite shore. I was happy in preventing the men from scalping even the Indians, being desirous, if possible, to teach even the savages humanity; but the men were much better employed, and kept in excellent order. We were out so long, that a number of British regulars, accompanied by what Indians, &c. could be rallied, had marched down to a thicket on the other side of the river, about 50 yards from the road we were to pass on our return; near this place I had ordered the field-piece;—the ambush was not quite formed when we discovered them, and gave them a well-directed fire. Here especially Major Bedlow with his field-piece did considerable execution.—Here also the enemy were annoyed by the fire of several cannon from the fort, as they marched round to form the ambuscade.—The enemy's fire was very wild, and though we were very much exposed, did no execution at all. We brought in four prisoners, three of which were wounded. One of the prisoners is a Mr. George Singleton of Montreal; he is a lieutenant in a company of which Mr. Stephen Watts, of New-York, (brother-in-law to Sir John Johnson,) was captain, and who was himself killed in the battle with the militia about two hours before. Mr. Singleton told me that Sir John Johnson was with him when we attacked their camp, and that he thinks he ran to the river. It is said by some of the Oneida Indians that he is killed, which does not appear unlikely. From these prisoners we received the first accounts of General Harkaman's militia being ambushed on their march; and of a severe battle they had with them about two hours before, which gave reason to think they had for the present given up their design of marching to the fort.

I should not do justice to the officers and soldiers who were with me on this enterprize, if I were not in the most positive terms to assure their countrymen that they in general behaved with the greatest gallantry upon this occasion; and next to the very kind and signal interposition of divine Providence which was powerfully manifested in their favour, it was undoubtedly owing to that noble intrepidity which discovered itself in this attack, and struck the enemy with such a panic as disenabled them from taking pains to direct their fire, *that we had not one man killed or wounded.* The officers in general behaved so well that it is hardly right to mention the name of any particular one for their singular valour: but, so remarkably intrepid was Captain Van Benscouton, and so rapid was his attack, that it demands from me this particular testimony of his extraordinary spirit.

Among other things taken from the enemy were several bundles of papers and a parcel of letters belonging to our garrison, which they had taken from our militia, but not yet opened; here I found one letter for myself; there were likewise papers belonging to Sir John Johnson and several others of the enemy's officers, with letters to and from General St. Leger, their commander; these papers have been of some service to us. On the evening of the next day the enemy fired a few cannon at us from high ground, about half a mile north of the fort, where they have erected a small battery. Next day, being Friday the 8th, they threw a parcel of shells from the same battery, none of which did any execution. This evening they sent us a flag, with which came their Adjutant General, Captain Armstrong, Colonel Butler, and a surgeon ; the surgeon to examine Singleton's wounds ; the principal business of the flag was to acquaint us that General St. Leger had with much difficulty prevailed on the Indians to agree that if the commanding officer would deliver up the fort, the garrison should be secured from any kind of harm, that not a hair of their heads should be touched, but if not, the consequence to the garrison, should it afterwards fall into their hands, must be terrible ; that the Indians were very much enraged on account of their having a number of their chiefs killed in the late action, and were determined, unless they got possession of the fort, to go down the Mohawk river and fall upon its inhabitants. Our answer was, that should this be the case, the blood of those inhabitants would be upon the heads of Mr. Butler and his employers, not upon us, and that such proceedings would ever remain a stigma upon the name of Britain ; but for our parts we were determined to defend the fort.

That evening it was agreed by the field officers that I should undertake with Lieutenant Stockwell, (who is a good woodsman,) to endeavour to get down into the country, and by making a proper representation of our affairs endeavour to procure such force as may be sufficient entirely to extirpate this miscreant band. After a most severe march of about 50 miles through the wilderness, I arrived at this place, and am in no doubt of beholding in a few days a force sufficient to accomplish this important piece of business. By the best accounts the loss of the Indians is very considerable, and they are quite sick of the expedition.

MARINUS WILLETT.

*German Flatts, August* 11, 1777.

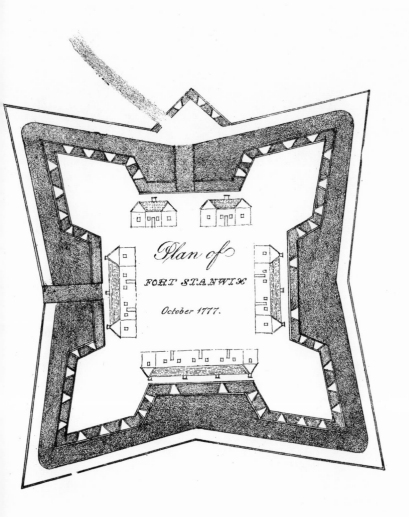

Plan of
FORT STANWIX
October 1777.

## No. V.

In commemoration of this sally, Congress ordered a sword to be presented to Colonel WILLETT.

IN CONGRESS, October 4, 1777.

Resolved, That Congress have a just sense of the distinguished merit of Lieutenant Colonel Willett, for a repeated instance of his bravery and conduct in his late successful sally on the enemy investing Fort Schuyler ; and that the commissary general of military stores be directed to procure an elegant sword, and present the same to Lieutenant Colonel Willett, in the name of these United States.

*By order of Congress,*
JOHN HANCOCK, President.

York Town, Pennsylvania, October 5th, 1777.

SIR,—I do myself the pleasure to transmit the enclosed resolve, in which you will perceive the sense of Congress, expressed in the highest terms of approbation, on your bravery and conduct, in the successful sally which you made on the enemy while they invested Fort Schuyler. In consideration of your behaviour and distinguished merit on that occasion, the Congress have directed the commissary general of military stores, to present you with an elegant sword, in the name and on behalf of the United States of America.

I have the honor to be, Sir,
Your most obedient servant,
JOHN HANCOCK, President.

*Col. Willett.*

To this Letter the following answer was returned :

SIR,—It is a peculiar pleasure to me to have the sword, directed by Congress to be presented me by the resolve of the 4th of October, 1777, delivered by a gentleman who has borne so conspicuous a share in the toils and honors of the late war. May your services in your present important office be as useful to your country in the closet as they have formerly been in the field.

With my best thanks for your kind wishes, I have the honor to be, with sentiments of the greatest respect and esteem, Sir, Your most obedient and humble servant,

MARINUS WILLETT.

*The Honorable Major General Knox, Secretary of War.*

---

## No. VI.

For this victory the Freedom of the City of Albany was presented to Colonel WILLETT.

At a Common Council held at the City Hall of the City of Albany, on the 19th day of July, 1781 :

Resolved, That the thanks of this Board be given to Col. Marinus Willett, and the officers and troops under his command, for their bravery, intrepidity, and military conduct in the action of the 10th instant, near Thurlough, in Tryon county, who, with an inferior force, defeated and put to flight the enemy under the command of Brandt and Frery.

Resolved, also, That the Freedom of this City, be presented to Col. Willett, in testimony of the high sense this Board entertain of his patriotism and distinguished merit.

Extract from the Minutes.

MAT. VISSCHER, Clerk.

GENTLEMEN,—I beg leave to offer you my warmest acknowledgments for your favorable sentiments of the conduct of the few gallant officers and soldiers engaged with me in the late action in Tryon county. This mark of your approbation must essentially increase the satisfaction they have already experienced of being instrumental in chastising a cruel and savage enemy, (the natural ally of the British King,) and will afford a rich compensation for the toils and difficulties they had to encounter.

I esteem myself much honored by your resolution of this date, and particularly by being admitted to the rights of a freeman in this ancient and respectable city. Be pleased to accept my thanks for your politeness on this occasion, and permit me at the same time to observe to you, gentlemen, that I wish never to sheath the sword I have early drawn in defence of American *liberty*, as long as there is a soldier or a savage in the service of Britain, in any part of the States of America.

I am, Gentlemen,

With the highest sentiments of respect and esteem,

Your most obedient

and humble servant,

MARINUS WILLETT.

Albany, 19th July, 1781.

*To the Worshipful the Mayor, Aldermen, and Commonalty of the City of Albany.*

## No. VII.

The following Extracts from different sources refer to this battle of Johnstown.

Extract from the New-York Journal and the General Advertiser, Monday, November 19th, 1781.

*Extracts from the Fishkill paper.*

" That the enemy, between six and seven hundred regulars, rangers, yagers, and Indians, under Major Ross, having advanced to Johnstown, were met by Col. Willett, defeated, and pursued into the wilderness, where many of them must probably have perished.—That Major Butler was among the slain of the enemy, and many prisoners, chiefly British, sent in. The General expresses the warmest thanks and highest sensibility of the address, gallantry, and persevering activity of Col. Willett ; and highly approves the conduct of the officers and soldiers in general, particularly of Major, the levies, and militia under his command, who at a critical moment, did honor to themselves, and rendered most essential service to their country."

Extracts from the New-York Packet and the American Advertiser. Fishkill, Wednesday, November 29th, 1731.

*Philadelphia, Nov. 15.*

*Head Quarters, Continental Village, Nov. 8th.*

Sir,—Since I had the honor of addressing your Excellency this morning, I have received the enclosed papers (referring to my father's official account of the battle) from Major General Lord Stirling, by which Congress will perceive that the enemy have been completely disappointed in their designs on the northern frontiers of this state, and defeated with considerable loss. The address, gallantry, and persevering activity exhibited by Col. Willett, on this occasion, do him the highest honor. The conduct of Major Rowley and the brave militia under his command, at a critical moment, merits particular commendations.

> I have the honor to be, with the highest respect,
> Your Excellency's most obedient servant,
> W. HEATH.

*His Excellency the President of Congress.*

Extract of a Letter from Major General Lord Stirling, dated Saratoga, November 6th, 1781.

" I have received a letter from Col. Willett, (the official account,) a copy of which is enclosed. The returns he alludes to, were never sent. The vigilant, prudent conduct of this officer, through the whole affair, was such as reflects the highest honor on the military character, and the essential service he has done his country, will give him a pleasing remembrance in every honest breast. The number he has taken, killed, and wounded, with the distressed situation in which he left them, will amount to little short of a total defeat. Eight days' march will scarcely bring them to a country where they can be supplied with provisions."

Extract of a Letter from Governor Clinton, dated Pokeepsie, 8th November, 1781.

" DEAR SIR,

" I am this moment favoured with yours of the 2d inst. and most sincerely congratulate you on your safe return to Fort Rensalaer, and your different successes over the enemy in Tryon county. I am sensible of the dangers and difficulties you had to encounter on this occasion ; and I am persuaded much is due to your personal exertions, and that nothing was wanting on your part to have ensured a complete victory ; and I trust the vigor with which the enemy was attacked, routed, and pursued, will be attended with the most salutary consequences to the frontier settlements."

* * *

## No. VIII.

The success of the Creek Mission is thus spoken of in Marshall's Life of Washington. Vol. 5th, page 273.

" For this service (i. e. the Creek Mission) Colonel Willett, a gallant and intelligent officer who had served through the war of the revolution, was selected ; and he acquitted himself so well of the duty assigned to him, that the chiefs of the nation, with M'Gillivray at their head, were induced to repair to New-York, where negotiations were immediately opened which terminated in a treaty of peace signed on the 7th day of August."

* * *

## No. IX.

*Correspondence of General Washington in relation to the Expedition against Oswego.*

### LETTER I.

" *Newburgh*, 18*th December*, 1782.

DEAR SIR,

Your letter of the 29th ult. from Albany, came safe to my hand. I am glad to find you enter so readily into a measure which appears very practicable in my eyes, provided the troops for the enterprise can be properly accommodated.

I have again written to the Secretary at War respecting clothing for the York state troops, and desired Colonel Tilhman, who left this on Sunday last for Philadelphia, to *enforce* it, not only on him, but on the clothier general also ; that, if it can be had, it may be sent up without delay. From the deputy clothier's store at this place, I could furnish vests and woollen hose enough for the State troops, and woollen caps, socks, and mittens sufficient for the whole party.

Indian shoes or moccasons I must depend upon you to procure, and also the snow shoes, of which I do not forsee the necessity for each man's having a pair, though some may be indispensably necessary. I well remember to have directed (two years ago,) a number of snow shoes to be made ; and if I mistake not it was done : but I do not suppose any dependance is to be had on them at this time. It may not be amiss however to inquire of General Schuyler (to whom I think I wrote on the subject) the quarter-master, or any other who may be likely to give information, whether they are yet in being.

To provide and carry scaling ladders from the settlement would at once announce your design, and more than probably defeat the enterprise—at any rate they would be troublesome to transport, and must impede the rapidity of your movements, on which every thing depends.—It appears to me therefore that the attempt would be improper, and that the difficulty may be surmounted by carrying a few tools, (to-wit, axes, saws, augers and a gouge) with which, at a convenient time and place, a sufficient number of ladders might easily be made.

The mode you propose for obtaining the sleighs and assembling the troops, I approve of preferably to the quarter-master's having any agency in the business, and do of the time named for the execution, if the clothing can be got to you in season ; but having doubts on this head, I shall be glad to know to how late a period the expedition can be delayed, on account of the ice on the Oneida Lake, and goodness of the sleighing.

If there be a *necessity* for a party to precede the sleighs a day or two to mark the route, it ought to consist of picked men, of tried fidelity, and even then the chance of discovery is greater than it otherwise would be.

The strength of *your* party should be proportioned to *that* of the garrison you attempt, for which reason every possible pains should be used to obtain the most accurate account of it. If you have men to set the enemy at defiance, in case of their discovering you previous to the assault or miscarriage therein, it is all that is necessary. More than these would render your movements unweildly and slow : consequently more liable to discovery in your preparation and on the march.

I should be glad to hear from you again on this head by some safe conveyance ; and if matters can be properly pre-pared for the enterprise, and nothing more than I know of at this time to hinder it, I will be at Albany when you march, that I may be at hand to remove difficulties if any should occur. With great esteem and regard,

I am, dear sir,

Your most obedient servant,

G. WASHINGTON.

*Col. Willett.*

P. S. It will be essentially necessary to fix your eyes upon some one or more persons (deserter or otherwise,) who have been in and are acquainted with the enemy's works, and seize them at the moment they are wanted that you may have them as guides."

## Letter II.

*Newburgh, January 22d, 1783.*

Dear Sir,—On the 20th, by your paymaster, I informed you, that besides the usual proportion of clothing, I had sent to your orders woollen caps, socks, and mitts, for the intended enterprise, to be made use of, or not, according to circumstances. —I have also written to Mr. Duer, who is now at Albany, to lay in a month's provisions for one hundred men, at each of the posts of Forts Rensselaer and Herkimer, and till further orders have placed the Rhode Island regiment under your direction.

For the reasons you assign, I approve of the time you propose for the attack, and suppose it will be necessary for you to begin your march from Fort Herkimer at the time you mention, viz. on the 8th or 9th of next month.

If the sleighing should be good, and business does not prevent it, I will endeavour to be at that place, or Fort Rensselaer by that time, but of this you will take no notice to *any body*, nor suffer it to have any influence on your preparations or conduct before or at the time, as many things may intervene to detain me.

All that remains to be done is now with you to do. And as the matter is between ourselves, and you have better information of the situation of the enemy, and difficulty in getting at them, than I,—I have only to request you to act from your best judgment, under a firm persuasion that if the enterprise in contemplation was even better known than it is, no imputation could fall upon you for having laid it aside, if the difficulties in the way should be greater than appeared

19

at first view. Let me hear from you, and if possible by the 3d or 4th of next month.

I am, dear sir,

Your most obedient servant,

G. WASHINGTON.

*Colonel Willett.*

———

## LETTER III.

*Newburgh, February 2d,* 1783.

DEAR SIR,—Your letters of the 28th ultimo from Fort Rensselaer, and 30th from Albany, both came to my hands last night.

One hundred and fifty blankets (all that are in the clothier's store at this place) and twenty-five axes, are now packing to be sent to you, and the Quartermaster-General will endeavour, if possible, to have them at Albany on the 4th, from whence you must take measures to get them to Fort Herkimer in time. If any of Olney's men (on the enterprize you are going) should be in greater need than yours, they must be supplied out of this parcel, that the whole may be as comfortable as it is in my power to make them.

I do not send medicines, bandages and instruments, because it would take some time to procure them, and not a moment is to be lost in dispatching the sleighs with the blankets, that they may arrive in time, and because (though I wish you not to be unprovided) it is to be remembered, and I wish to impress it upon you, that if you do not succeed by surprize, the attempt will be unwarrantable. The wounds received in the former, more than probable, will be trifling.

Every plausible deception should be used to mask the object of your expedition to the latest moment. Your movements afterwards should be quick, and pains must be taken to discover, by tracks or otherwise, whether intelligence has outgone you.—If you should be fully convinced of this, the further prosecution of the enterprize would not only be fruitless, but might prove injurious.

To an officer of your care, attention and foresight, I shall not dwell upon circumspection and caution. The consequence of a surprize, (not only to the party you command, but to your own reputation,) is too serious and self-evident, to stand in need of illustration. A vast deal depends upon having good guides to Oswego; and every thing, in a manner, upon persons that can carry you without hesitation and difficulty to the points of attack, when you arrive there.

How far a few Indians would be useful to you for the first purpose ; and how far they are to be confided in, you, from a better knowledge of them than I possess, must judge, and act accordingly.

Guides who are pressed in the service must be well secured, lest they desert from you in a critical moment.

From having recourse to the almanack, I am led to wish that the night for the attack may not be delayed beyond the 12th inst. ; as I find that the setting of the moon, (even at that time,) approaches so near day-light, that the intervening space is short, and consequently must be very critical ; as accidents unforeseen, and consequently unprovided for, may embarrass your movements towards the works, and retard the attack of them beyond the hour designed, to the entire disappointment of the plan : Let me caution you, therefore, against being too exact in your                              of time for your last movement—reflect that you can always waste time, but never recover it. Halts, or slow marching, will accomplish the first ; but nothing can effect the latter—consequently, in such an enterprize as yours, want of time will be a certain defeat.

Let your disposition be such, that in any circumstances your retreat to your sleighs, and afterwards with them, may be secure.

If success should crown your endeavours, let your first object be to secure your prisoners, whom you will treat with lenity and kindness ; suffering no insult or abuse to be offered them with impunity, your next object must be to destroy the works ; the vessels (if any should be found there) and every thing else which cannot be brought away. Such works as cannot be consumed by fire, nor easily erased by the soldiers, must be, if practicable, blown up. In a word, they are to be effectually demolished, if it is within the compass of your power to do it.

Whatever is found in, or about the works, belonging to the enemy, and is agreeable to the rules and customs of war, humanity and generosity, shall be given to the party as the reward of their gallantry and fatigue—to be distributed in proportion to their pay. The drivers of sleighs, if countrymen, should receive a part as an extra encouragement for their services.

Make me the earliest report, (if successful, from the scene of action—at any rate on your return,) of your progress, and the issue of the expedition. The inclosed letter will show you what I have done respecting spirits and subsistence for your officers. Seal it before delivery, and make your arrangements with the contractor. I begin to doubt the practicability of my being up ; my sentiments however you are possessed of, as well as the aid I can give. Your own judgment must govern where my instructions are deficient. I heartily wish you honour and success, and am

Dear Sir, your most obedient servant,

G WASHINGTON.

*Colonel Willett.*

## LETTER IV.

*Head Quarters, 5th March, 1783.*

SIR,—I have been favoured with your letter of the 19th of February, announcing the failure of your attempt against Oswego.

Unfortunate as the circumstance is, I am happy in the persuasion that no imputation or reflection can justly reach your character; and that you are enabled to derive much consolation from the animated zeal, fortitude, and activity of the officers and soldiers who accompanied you. The failure, it seems, must be attributed to some of those unaccountable events which are not within the control of human means; and which, though they often occur in military life, yet require, not only the fortitude of the soldier, but the calm reflection of the philosopher to bear.

I cannot omit expressing to you the high sense I entertain of your persevering exertions and zeal on this expedition; and beg you to accept my warm thanks on the occasion; and that you will be pleased to communicate my gratitude to the officers and men who acted under your command, for the share they had in that service.

With much esteem and regard,

I am, Sir,

Your most obedient servant,

G. WASHINGTON.

*Lieut. Col. M. Willett.*

---

## No. X.

*Meeting of Citizens in the Park, Wednesday, August 10, 1814.*

### PUBLIC MEETING.

On Wednesday, pursuant to public notice, there assembled in the Park, in front of the City Hall, an immense concourse of citizens. Colonel Henry Rutgers, was unanimously called to the Chair, and Oliver Wolcott, Esquire, appointed Secretary. They took their stations in the centre balcony. Col. Willett, standing near the Chairman, and the flag of the nation waving over his head, delivered an address to his fellow-citizens, well calculated to inspire animation and courage.

He began by asking the indulgence of his fellow-citizens for the talk of an old man.—He then proceeded:—

Threescore and fourteen years have brought with them some bodily infirmities—had it been otherwise, and that my strength of body had remained as unimpaired as my love for my country, and the spirit that still animates me, you would not, my friends, have seen me here this day: I should have been amongst that glorious band, that, on the waters of Erie and Ontario, have achieved so much fame and lasting glory for their country!

A life of seventy-four years has afforded me opportunities of seeing many great and surprising changes.

Fifty-eight years are now passed since I was a witness of press-gangs traversing these streets, and dragging men from their houses on board of ships of war! What a contrast between that time and this! Let those now reflect upon it, who, instead of thanking that kind Providence which delivered us from such oppressive domination, employ their whole power to weaken and subvert a government made by ourselves, and for ourselves—the fruit of our blood and toil! What spirit is this, that, in the present crisis of our country, can lead to measures so disgraceful? Shall we abuse and vilify those men we have placed at the head of our affairs, because they do not act just as we are pleased to say they should? Are we, for that reason, to refuse compliance with the laws of our country? No, my fellow-citizens! for it is justly stated in the address of the Common Council, that we are not, in the present situation of our country, to inquire into the wisdom of the measures which resulted in the declaration of this war.  It is a fact, that we are at war; and that that war has been undertaken agreeably to the constitution of our country. Every man bound to support the constitution of the United States, is, therefore, bound to support the war—because it is a constitutional act, and such is the law of the land.  But, had I power to detail, and you patience to hear, what I have known and observed of the haughty, cruel, and gasconading nation that makes war against us, your feelings would outstrip my words, and anticipate the voice and commands of authority.  The terms I use towards our enemy are not mine alone, nor proceeding from the personal warmth of my individual character.  Such were the sentiments of men as great as this or any nation can boast of—Washington and Franklin.  Dr. Franklin delivered his opinions in his correspondence with Lord Howe ; and those of General Washington I have had from his own lips.

Forty years ago I was at a meeting of citizens assembled on this green.  The acclamation then was "*join or die.*" The unanimity of that day procured the repeal of some obnoxious laws ; but the design of enslaving us was not relinquished.  Troops were stationed throughout the colonies to carry the nefarious intention into execution.  Many were the broils between the citizen and the soldier, for the spirit of the citizens was roused, and they viewed with just indignation, the mercenary troops that were to overthrow their liberties.  They were stung by the ingratitude of the nation to which they had yielded loyal obedience, and assisted in its wars with ardour and alacrity  But had the enemy then conquered us as we did them, how different would have been our situation at this day ! Reflecting on this, it seems to me almost incredible that there should be Americans that could espouse the cause of such an enemy. Of what stuff are such hearts made ? Is it possible that any such should be amongst the sons of those who fought your battles, my fellow-citizens, and won your freedom.

It was, in the war of the revolution, a favourite toast—"May every Citizen be a Soldier, and every Soldier a Citizen."

Our citizens must now again become soldiers, and those soldiers be good citizens—not parading soldiers, fellow-citizens, but fighting soldiers—soldiers willing and ready to encounter the hardships and fatigues of war. I am not what I have been ; but such as I am, wherever the enemy seek to deal most destruction, there you may look for me. And as to this mistaken idea, that American militia are unequal to the contest with British regulars, I am a living witness to the contrary. With militia I have encountered them. I have met them when their numbers were double mine ; and I have routed and pursued them. You, my fellow-citizens, if you will, can do the same. There is no terror in them for brave men, who dare look them in the face, and lock the bayonet with them. Let those who would dismay you by the terrors of war, rather reflect upon the part they have had in encouraging your enemy; and though war, like pestilence, may have been visited upon nations for their crimes, yet against this enemy we have committed no offence. We bore with the cruelty, injustice and oppression of that insolent nation, till it became insupportable.

Instead, therefore, of cavilling at the measures or operations of the war, let us rather unite to banish envy, hatred and discord, from amongst us ; and resolve with all our might, to resist that implacable enemy, who will never respect us till we again compel him so to do.

Permit me, then, my dear fellow-citizens, to conclude with a chorus we were used to sing in the camp in days of much more danger:

> Let Europe empty all her force,
> We'll meet them in array,
> And shout—Huzza—Huzza—Huzza,
> For Life and Liberty.

[This pithy discourse from a tried and truly statesman of the revolution, whose acts were vouchers for his words, had its full effect, and was cheered with unbounded applause.]

---

## No. XI.

*Extracted from the Speech of Col. Willett as Chairman of the Greek Committee.*

"Upwards of fourscore and three years having rendered me incapable of the activity requisite as Chairman of this Committee, I am induced to desire to be excused from attendance on its deliberations. The cause of the Greeks is undoubtedly the cause of liberty. The first of last month was fifty-eight years since I was actively engaged with the sons of liberty in this city, in opposing the first attempts made by the British government to enslave our country by introducing the memorable stamp act. On the night in which it was to have been put into execution, I was employed in preparing, exhibiting, and burning the effigies of those persons who were most noted in producing that act. 'Join or die,' was echoed through our streets. It was a glorious night."

Col. Willett then proceeded to make some remarks in relation to the causes which produced the revolutionary war; and to the general diffusion of liberal principles since that eventful period. He then closed in the following manner :—

"Permit me, as the only help I can at present bestow, to offer two thousand acres of land due to me from the state of New York, become my due agreeably to a law passed by the legislature of the state of New York, in March 1781, by defending the frontiers in the campaigns of 1781, 1782, 1783 : which were by far the most arduous of any that I served during the war of the revolution. There was more fatigue, more hazard and anxiety in one of those campaigns than in seven such as I served in the year 1789, with the army under the immediate command of General Washington."

---

## No. XII.

The following are from among the numerous tributes of respect paid to the memory of Col. Marinus Willett.

*New York State Society of Cincinnati.*

*New York, August 23, 1830.*

The President, with deep and sincere regret, announces to the members of the Society, the death of their venerable and esteemed friend and brother, Col. Marinus Willett, who departed this life last evening.

Col. Willett commenced his military career in the colonial service of the British government, in the reign of George the 2d; was actively engaged on the northern and western frontiers of this state in the (French) war of 1756, and was present at the battle of Oswego, where the first Lord Howe was killed. Upon the breaking out of the war of the Revolution, Col. Willett joined the standard, and entered the service of his country, in which it was his good fortune to be highly distinguished and useful : he was a volunteer at the battle of Monmouth on the 28th of June, 1778, when the British forces, under General Sir Henry Clinton, were defeated : he was eminently distinguished in the siege of Fort Stanwix, and also at the battle of Johnstown, (Montgomery county,) on the 25th of October, 1781, in both of which he commanded.

Col. Willett continued in the revolutionary army until the close of the war of independence, commanding at that time the 5th regiment : he was remarkable for personal bravery, military enterprise, and energy of purpose.

In private life, Col. W. was one of the most amiable of men, and after the war held several civil offices ; the last of which was the mayoralty of this city.

The members of the Society are directed to wear the usual badge of mourning in honour of Col. Willett for thirty days ; they are also respectfully invited to attend the funeral of their deceased companion, to-morrow (Tuesday) afternoon, at half-past 4 o'clock, from his late residence, No. 58 Broome street, between Cannon and Lewis streets.

By order of Col. RICHARD VARICK, President.

CHAS. GRAHAM, Secretary.

*\*\* Carriages for the members of the Society will be in attendance in front of the City Hall at 4 o'clock.

---

### First Division New York State Artillery.
#### DIVISION ORDERS.
##### New York, August 23, 1830.

Information has been given to the major-general of the death of Col. Marinus Willett, who departed this life last evening, at the advanced age of ninety years.

Providence appears to have continued to a late day several of those patriots who served our country in the cabinet and in the field during the revolutionary war, as it were to reward them with witnessing and enjoying the happiness which their councils or their valour acquired, and by their presence to keep alive the principles by which they led their country to freedom and independence.

Few men have sunk to the tomb more entitled to the gratitude and respect of their countrymen, than Colonel Willett.

He was among the early assertors of our country's rights, and his conduct in defence of Fort Stanwix, and the perilous hazards he encountered in bringing relief to the garrison, are among the most brilliant feats of the war.

Such men the country delight to honour when living, and to cherish their memory when dead.

The Corps of Artillery are ever ready to pay honours to military departed worth.

The major general therefore directs Brigadier General Spicer to order the regiment commanded by Colonel Sanford, Brigadier General Arcularius to order a squadron of cavalry from his brigade, and Brigadier General Hopkins to order a battalion of artillery from his brigade, to perform the military honours at the interment of the deceased.

The corps from General Spicer's and General Arcularius' brigades, will parade at 4 o'clock, P. M. at the late residence of Colonel Willett, corner of Broome and Lewis streets. The battalion from General Hopkins' brigade will form on the Battery at 4 o'clock, P. M. and will fire minute-guns from that place, corresponding in numbers with the age of the deceased. The whole detachment will be under the command of Colonel Sanford.

General Hopkins will order the flag to be hoisted at the Battery, at half-mast, from sunrise and during the day.

General Muir will, on requisition, issue the necessary ammunition.

The officers of the Division not on duty are invited to attend the funeral.

By order of Major General Morton.

S. D. JACKSON,
Colonel and Division Inspector.

————

*From the New York Daily Advertiser.*

Died, in this city, on Sunday evening last, Col. Marinus Willett, in the 91st year of his age. Col. Willett was an officer of distinguished merit through the war of Independence; and has enjoyed in a high degree the respect and confidence of his fellow-citizens and the community. A more particular account of the life and character of this venerable patriot and soldier, will doubtless be prepared and published by some person more intimately acquainted with the events of his long and honourable life.

————

*From the New-York Commercial.*

*Col. Willett.*—We hastily noticed yesterday, as our paper was going to press, the death of this venerable soldier of the revolution, whose public services are matters of history, and who has been most happy in his private life ; enjoying in good old age the esteem of all around him, the possession of all his faculties, and the consolations of religious faith and hope. The public testimonies of respect which will be paid to his memory were never more honourably deserved.

*From the New-York Mirror.*

*Colonel Marinus Willett.*—This veteran officer of the Revolution died on Sunday, the 23d instant, in the ninety-first year of his age. On Tuesday his remains were deposited in their final resting-place, with civil and military honours, attended by a vast concourse of citizens, with numerous friends and relatives, who better knew the worth, and of course more deeply felt the deprivation which all lamented. The character of the deceased needs not the feeble eulogy of our pen. His biography is inseparably interwoven with the history of our country's glory.

———

*From the Courier and Enquirer.*

In the personal character of Colonel Willett, there were traits of chivalry and daring, so fearless and ardent, that in another age he would have commanded the deepest and greatest admiration. The present generation is perhaps even too near the Revolution to give due honor and respect to the heroic characters which that great event produced. Alas! what now are our patriots—our sages—our lovers of country, when compared with the men of the revolution! Selfishness covers and influences every action—private interest usurps the place of public good. How different were these sainted men! What fearlessness! what openness! what candour! in every act that their country required of them. They had no thought of self during that momentous struggle. Look at Carroll, nursed in wealth and ease, risking every thing, every pleasure, and all the means of quiet happiness, for the glory and independence of his country! See Willett! meeting death in every shape—braving all dangers to establish that liberty which we are now enjoying. The Revolution was the age that gave souls to men's bosoms.

*From the New-York Constellation.*

*Death of Colonel Willett.*—Another Revolutionary soldier is gone. The venerable Colonel Willett died on Sunday evening, at his house, Cedar Grove, in the 91st year of his age. He was a lieutenant in the French war, and a colonel in the war of the Revolution. He distinguished himself by his defence at Fort Stanwix against the united attacks of the British and Indian marauders. His courage and presence of mind were particularly displayed in his conflicts with the sons of the forest.—In private life Col. Willett was distinguished for integrity, frankness, and decision of character.

———

*From the New-York Herald.*

*Death of Col. Willett.*—We have to record the demise of this brave soldier of the Revolution, generally known as "the Hero of Fort Stanwix." Col. Willett not only claimed admiration for his valour, but the confidence of his fellow citizens, in numerous public stations, which he filled with honour. He died at a good old age, which was cheered by the recollections of a life spent in the service of his country, and the respect and veneration of all around him. Being unprepared to give a sketch of his life, we copy the following notice of his decease from the Evening Post:—

*From the New-York Evening Post.*

The venerable Colonel Willett is no more. He died last evening at his house, Cedar Grove, in the 91st year of his age. Col. Willett distinguished himself by his bravery and good conduct in the war of the Revolution. His courage, prowess and presence of mind, were particularly displayed in conflicts with the Indians who took part w h Great Britain.

He was a man of great integrity, frankness, and decision of character in private life. We could wish some person acquainted with the events of his life would furnish a sketch of them for this paper.

————

*From the Albany Daily Advertiser.*

### THE NEW-YORK LINE.

Few troops behaved with more bravery during the Revolution, than the *New-York Line,* as they were called. An ardent devotion to the great cause, impelled them to the most heroic achievements. An unfading lustre remains upon their history. After a thousand years have passed, said Chateaubriand, the chivalry of the North American patriots will be sung by some future Ossian on the banks of the Superior.

The natural position of New-York rendered it a scene of the most important military events. Its extent of territory, and contiguity to Canada, rendered its possession and defence a theme for Washington often to speculate upon. The most glorious and spirit-stirring recollections of the revolution, are associated with the name of every river, mountain and valley in the State. The thunders from Fort Putnam reverberated over the highlands of the Hudson; while the recesses of the forests echoed at Fort Stanwix with the musketry of its brave defenders. It devolved upon Washington to commit this northern frontier to a Spartan band. He selected from the honest descendants of the Dutch emigrants, a chosen corps. To them he committed the destinies of this section of the republic, well assured of its security and protection. For when his southern staff volunteered to march on to the north to arrest the triumphant progress of Burgoyne, he replied to them, that he had no apprehensions for the north—that there was a *belt of oak* there, that would secure it from British invasion. With Richard he might have exclaimed,

> " What do they in the north,
> When they should serve their sovereign in the west ?"

It was Schuyler and Gates, Van Schaick, Gansevoort, Willett, Rutgers, and others, who wrested this fair sister from the rude grasp of foreign intruders. They formed a *belt of oak*—a bond of union, a phalanx of power, abounding in virtue, courage and patriotism. Well did Pitt observe in Parliament to the tory party, "that with prophetic vision he saw the catastrophe which awaited the British power in the colonies. They had no Washington, or Adams, or Hancock there for nought."

———

### From the *Albany Evening Journal.*

The venerable Marinus Willett, terminated his long, useful, and honourable life, on Sunday evening, at his residence in Broome-street, New-York. Col. Willett had attained his 90th year. Virtue, philanthropy and patriotism, guided every step, and adorned every act of his lengthened and eventful life. He was a gallant and distinguished soldier, during the Revolutionary war, and has held various and honourable public stations under the state and national governments.

———

### From the *Rochester Daily Advertiser.*

The venerable Col. Marinus Willett, died at his residence in New York on Sunday last in his 90th year, He was one of those, who in the stormy period which "tried men's souls," perilled all for his country, and lived long to rejoice in its independence. He has been gathered in a truly " good old age " to his fathers, and has left a name that will brighten in the estimation of posterity.

---

*From the Troy Sentinel.*

Another hero of the revolution, Col. Marinus Willett, aged 91, departed to his last rest on Sunday evening, at his residence at Cedar Grove, New York. He was throughout the Revolution an active and useful officer, and in his latter years has been uniformly honoured as an excellent citizen, and beloved as an estimable man.

---

*Funeral of Col. Willett.*—The Common Council of New-York have passed resolutions of respect to Col. Willett, and will attend his funeral as a public body. He will be buried with military honors. The State Society of the Cincinnati will be mourners on the occasion, and the military will be from the First Division of Artillery. The Court of Errors and other public bodies will join the procession.

> " Such honours Ilion to her heroes paid,
> And peaceful slept the mighty Hector's shade."

THE END.